# Vocal Magick

## The User Friendly Guide to Your Most Adaptable Ritual Tool

# Vocal Magick

## The User Friendly Guide to your Most Adaptable Ritual Tool

## Bill Duvendack

Megalithica Books
**Stafford England**

**Vocal Magick: The User Friendly Guide to Your Most
Adaptable Ritual Tool**
**By Bill Duvendack**
© 2015 First edition

Editor: Kiya ScorryBreac
Copy Editor: Faring Forth
Layout: Taylor Ellwood
Cover Design: Isis Sousa

ISBN: 978-1-905713-99-8
MB0173

A Megalithica Books Publication
An imprint of Immanion Press

info@immanion-press.com
http://www.immanion-press.com

# Dedication

This book is dedicated to those that have supported me over the years, from family members to the person I don't know that has learned from me and is empowered by the experience.

# Table of Contents

# Introduction

Is reality language? Is what we know of the universe defined by language? If there were no spoken languages in the world, would we perceive reality as we do now? Would a hawk still be a hawk? What if each person spoke a different language? If that were true, there would be no language families, and thus no commonalties. Would that unweave the interconnected tapestry of human life? Would it strengthen individuality while hindering community? Would it do both? Would it do neither? Ack! Chaos, some would say!

In this book I'm going to take a look at the magickal connotations and occult meanings that usually go unnoticed within many linguistic ideas. I will challenge those open enough to constantly consider redefining their paradigm. What is in these pages is meant as a guideline to consider and to use in daily life to enhance the magickal experience of physical form. The concepts are ones that usually go unheard, or at least unattended to, by even the professionals within the field, so don't feel daunted if they are tough to grasp, or too massive to undertake all at once. Beware of the changes you open yourself to when you dare to ask yourself the questions I propose. This is neither for the faint of heart, nor for those insecure in their karma.

Ever since the beginning of time, humans have tried to verbally communicate with fellow humans. From the stereotypical grunts of cavemen in Hollywood 'B' movies, to the simplistic humor of "Me Tarzan, you Jane", it is well documented that there has always been a desire in the human race to communicate. Over the course of thousands of years this has evolved into what is commonly known today as language, which is classed into language families. However, these verbal attempts are, at their roots, different combinations of vibrations, and as such, have differing impacts on our perceptions of the universe and the shared experience of life. Throughout history there have been many languages, and not all have survived the test of time, but all have contributed to what we call "history", also known in some circles as "his story", which is known to predominantly be written by the victors. Even languages which are now unspoken, like ancient Egyptian hieroglyphics, have contributed to what we remember of what has come before. In this book I am going to demonstrate the lost art of communication, and show why, in this new aeon of changing energies, it is more necessary now than in two thousand years to be precise in speech and communication.

Now, if you dare, open your mind to what lies in these pages, knowing full well that what I lay before you is meant to challenge and stimulate your mind, the true birthplace of language.

Cheers,

Wm. Duvendack
St Louis MO

# Chapter 1
# Language: A Brief Overview

Is reality language? Questions like this one are common in the halls of higher learning globally, mostly discussed and debated by sociologists, anthropologists, and, to a lesser extent, psychologists. But, let us look at that simple question more closely: "I-s r-e-a-l-i-t-y l-a-n-g-u-a-g-e?" Seventeen letters. Seventeen, the number of the tarot trump The Star. Eight consonants, eight vowels, and one letter (y) that can go either way, depending on circumstance. Now that we've micromanaged it, let's take it the other way: Three words. In the grand scheme of the English language, a three word sentence is miniscule, but not as miniscule as the simple philosopher's quandary of "Why?" The above sentence might suggest that the issue we are going to address is three times as complex as what a philosopher would address if he were to address "why?" Of that three-fold complexity, one is going to be very esoteric in nature (that being the first word "is"; non-coincidentally the first two letters of the goddess Isis), the second word, "reality," is going to be very pragmatic and practical (Reality, is, after all, the illusion that our limited five senses perceive every day), and the third word, "language," is what this book is going to address.

### Ancient Roots

No one really knows when spoken language began. In recent times, a popular date for the beginning point for language is 50,000 years ago[1]. Considering that the last ice age is generally known to be about 10,000 years ago, this

---

[1] *The Science Times Book of Language and Linguistics*, edited by Nicholas Wade, The Lyons Press, 2000.

means that language has been around since way before what is commonly accepted in scientific circles as the modern era, which began at said ice age. However, if you subscribe to the Christian viewpoint that the modern era is post-life of Christ, then 50,000 years ago seems almost unfathomable. To put that into context, 50,000 years ago is the equivalent of about two years in the greater cycles of the Earth as it relates to the stars. There are fossils that date back millions of years. The zodiacal year – defined by the precession of the equinoxes and known as "Axis Precession" in astronomy, the rhythm by which each constellation takes its turn rising at the first of spring – is approximately 26,000 years long, which means two zodiacal years ago, roughly, language was created! Two zodiacal years; that's all! When you view language through this lens, 50,000 years ago seems recent. One might say it seems a conservative estimate, considering the fact that human remains date back thousands of years before that.

It is also believed that there was one proto-language that all others sprang from, and that one mother tongue is responsible for the rest as humanity migrated due to environmental and social factors. Could this be the reason for the story of the Tower of Babel in the Judeo-Christian Bible? Conceptually, yes, this could be the case. Logic would say that is an accurate and conceivable assessment. The number of vibratory sounds a person can theoretically make with their voice box and vocal cords is immense; however, there is a limited range that can be created in practice due to physical limitations. Further, we stop being able to perceive and produce the differences between certain sounds if they are not used in the languages that surround us! For example, in different languages in the world there are different sounds made and application of letters, and unless we are exposed to them on a regular basis, they may sound different until we get used to hearing them. The Asiatic language family is the most distinctive, but examples can be found in many different language. The Polish language has three different forms of the letter 'z', for example. There is also a limitation to what we can hear for the same reasons. Dogs, after all, have a more acute hearing sense than humans and can hear things far beyond the pitch that humans can perceive or reliably produce. When you blow into a dog whistle, most of the time you cannot hear the pitch, but dogs react to it, as it hurts their ears. We need a tool to make a pitch that irritates dogs; we cannot make that pitch on our own. Of course, it goes without saying that there are many other things that we can do that dogs can't, and thus the separation of the species, but I digress.

In essence, therefore, we have one proto-language 50,000 years ago that has given birth to the many languages that humanity has experienced since then, both still living and now defunct. To put it bluntly, there is one root that has given birth to everything we speak today. Very fairy tale like; very Adam and Eve fairy tale like, specifically, and yet very reasonable. Depending on what you believe and what you have read, you may have come across several different proposed homelands for this prototype language. I'm reminded of four different points of origin: The mythological Garden of Eden, Atlantis, Mesopotamia, and ancient Egypt. I'm sure that there are other ancient places that are rumored to be the source of this mother tongue, but there is no verifiable way to discover where, exactly, it came from. The most common and most hotly debated belief is that this originated out of Africa, but research is still being done on this. This hypothesis of one language 50,000 years ago will be the working model I will use in this text, however, so if you have a differing viewpoint, please keep this difference of perspective in mind while reading and adjust accordingly.

There is a scientific fact to ponder, though, which is the fact that Occam's Razor dictates that if there was one prototypical language, then it came from one spot on the planet, and thus it spread out from that single point. Even if some of these groups of people included nomads that then ventured elsewhere to plant those linguistic seeds in human populations that had not come up with language yet, everyone who spoke was still, at some point, at a central point.

The most reasonable assumption about how this occurred would be that a collection of people in the same geographical area at the same time needed to learn new ways to communicate their ideas more clearly. Following through with this line of thinking, it could suggest that language and its use came from an urban environment of some type, certainly one with a significant population density for the species at the time. It takes the exchange of ideas to bring about such a renaissance, and thus hints at language construction being one of the biggest innovations during a very transitional time for the human species.

Some could cite the 100th Monkey Syndrome, which is also entirely possible. For those of you that don't know what this is, let me explain it briefly. The 100th monkey syndrome is, in essence, the observation that when a certain number of beings of a particular related group absorb a new behavior, it mysteriously spreads to all members of that related group in ways that are currently unquantifiable when it comes to our ability to study them. As an example, to grossly and generically paraphrase the study, it was noted that when a certain group of monkeys performed a new behavior, this behavior spread to monkeys that were not present nor in contact with this initial group. The method of transmission was, and still is, unknown to modern scientific thought, although methods can be pondered. For a more detailed assessment of this concept, I suggest the following works: "Rhythms of

Vision," by Lawrence Blair, 1975, and "Lifetide," by Lyall Watson, 1979. It is not my intent to get into a great debate nor a great detailing of this study, but I do encourage you to investigate for your own knowledge. I simply share this idea here to explore the possibilities of the origins of language.

It is possible that language was transmitted in a way that is still not understood by modern science. Part of the theory behind the 100th monkey syndrome has to do with critical mass, which basically means that when enough of a group learns something, it then spreads to the remainder of the group through unknown means. Interestingly enough this is a chemistry principle, too. The concept of critical mass is something that has been worked with extensively in groups of modern spirituality over the last fifty years, as groups across the world have gathered together to pray or meditate for a particular result from their actions. Take, for example, World Peace Day. This has been occurring for the last few decades, and is a time during which groups and individuals have synchronized their efforts to pray and meditate for world peace across the globe. Part of the reason that they do this is that they believe if enough people participate in this, then world peace will be achieved as the idea of peace will spread across the globe in a manner similar to the 100th monkey syndrome. This highlights how infectious and insidious ideas and language truly are, and by being aware of this, we put ourselves in a more empowered position to affect change not only when it comes to individual conversations, but also with humanity as a whole.

While language may have been created roughly 50,000 years ago, it has not always included a written component. When written language was first created, it was mostly to keep oral traditions alive, and was based around pictures such as what is found in Nascaux, France. Pictographs, however, do not have a necessary correlation between image and sound, and are in their most extreme cases not fully translatable by anyone other than the author or artist. Also, in the case of extreme weather, a natural force could wash the pictures away, be it melting ice or a strong rain, unless grooves were carved underneath the medium used to "ink" them. This of course is where a lot of the stone artwork is found, especially in Central and South America. However, that could still be hindered by such events as earthquakes and landslides. There are other issues, though, that come into play, such as the use of color in primitive art.

After extended use of cave drawings, colors were added to show differences. For example, a golden calf would mean one thing, while a black calf would mean something else entirely. If there was an extreme weather scenario, like for example, an ice age, then there was a good chance that the "inks" would wash off, and all that would be left would be the foundation grooves of the letters, or the outlines of the artwork, and the next viewers of the picture would miss a great deal of its meaning. This would in turn only convey a fraction of the intended message. That's a pretty major problem if the tribe that left the artwork was trying to convey a warning of local disease to newcomers! All of a sudden the concept of communication has become difficult, and we're just dealing with drawings and their elaborations at this point. Wait until we hit the meat of the subject later in this book!

These sorts of texts evolved along with humanity, and logographic scripts such as the hieroglyphs of Ancient Egypt developed, where individual symbols could represent syllables, letters, or occasionally be read pictographically. One of the drawbacks of these languages is that they are not as easily transported, or, as in the case of hieroglyphs, not very easily understood by outsiders, though the difficulty in deciphering such language may in fact be considered a benefit by the people writing things down. Syllabaries such as Japanese represent language in terms of full syllables, and thus work best for languages that are much more regular in form than English, which is written in an alphabetic script. Whew! Writing things down is complicated, isn't it?

## Hebrew, Sanskrit, and Egypt's Bridge to Both

As humanity evolved, more complex ideas needed to be conveyed and in a shorter amount of time than it would take to create an artistic representation. Spoken language developed and is still developing in many forms to this day, and it came with its own esoteric beliefs about the meaning and nature of sound and language. The Hindus believe that the Om represents the seed sound that the universe is built on. This one primal sound can be combined with many other sounds, and thus the combination can affect the illusionary world we interact with everyday. In a nutshell, this is the theory behind mantras. The full story would be a whole other book[2]. However, the Om as the seed sound of the universe is going to be integral to the rest of this book. Why? The Hindu belief system is one of the oldest on the planet, and, as the occult author Dion Fortune has pointed out: "The nearer the source, the purer the stream". Therefore, it stands to reason that they have withstood the test of time. Mantras have, in recent years, seen a resurgence in use outside of India. Let's play devil's advocate for a moment, though, and let's say that the Om is NOT the seed sound of creation. However, Hindu doctrine suggests one important concept, which is that at the base of everything that has manifested there is a primal and foundational sound. Many scientists have explored this over the years, so there are sufficient resources available for those that choose to pursue this further.

---

[2] For more information, see *Healing Mantras* by Thomas Ashley-Farrand.

Hebrew also explores this concept, though in a much different fashion. According to the Qabala, the language has three "mother letters" that are its basis and which have been used magickally for several hundred years within the cultural context of the Jewish people. The three mother letters are Aleph, Mem, and Shin[3]. These three letters are, mystically speaking, the triad that generates the rest of their 22-letter alphabet. Hebrew also developed the idea that not only do letters have sounds that form speakable words, but also numerical definitions as well as esoteric and symbolic ones. For example, Aleph has a value of 1, and means "ox". In addition to these meanings, each Hebrew letter is written as a holy symbol. This is exemplified by one letter that they believe to be present in every other letter, which is the letter Yod. It is said that each Hebrew letter contains a Yod, and thus we have the indwelling of spirit in each manifested sound. All of a sudden you have an alphabet that can be strung together not only to convey thoughts, but also to convey numerical messages overtly or covertly, or encode whole-word meanings of the individual letters themselves. Almost a duality of sorts, but I like to think of it as a velvet glove cast in iron.

So why do I mention Hebrew now immediately after Sanskrit? Sanskrit is several thousand years old, and I believe that Hebrew is just as old, with a different point of origin, but most likely originating as a spoken language at close to the same time as Sanskrit. Archaeological research places these origin points at approximately 1700 BCE for Sanskrit, and 1,000 BCE for Hebrew. Sanskrit originated in Tibet, while Hebrew originated (get ready, this is where challenging notions begin) in Egypt. This can be debated, obviously, but there is so much evidence to suggest this as fact rather than theory. People have speculated that

---

[3] *777 and other Qabalistic Writings of Aleister Crowley*, Weiser Books, reprinted 1973.

written Hebrew related to the ancient Egyptian written language. It is believed that one of the inventions of written language was in Mesopotamia, but whether this was the sole origin point in the Eastern Hemisphere is unknown. It is not debatable that Mesopotamia had some of the earliest examples of written language that are found on the planet.

For example, the most common and well-known holy book in the West, the Bible, expounds on this, unwittingly so, in the Old Testament, when the Hebrew plight is discussed (See, among others, the book of Exodus). There is very little discussion of the language of the twelve tribes of Israel before this period of residence in Egypt, but when they leave the sands of the Egyptian empire, they have at their disposal a language that is one of the most, if not the most, advanced in the world at that time. Ergo it stands to reason that the development of Hebrew came during their period of residency of the twelve tribes of Israel in the land of milk and honey, and most likely was shaped by the influence of the Egyptians. Both Egyptian and Hebrew are in the Afroasiatic family of languages, though evidence suggests that Egyptian diverged from the Semitic language branch early on. In any event, Hebrew was born during a transitional time for the Hebrew people under the guidance of the Pharaohs. This puts it as not only one of the most thought out and complex languages still used in this day, but it also makes it one of the oldest in the world. It could be argued that it could go in its own category of one of the oldest languages still in use, though that is due to its modern reconstruction and revival rather than persistent usage through the centuries. Both it and Sanskrit are used today and have evolved over time from their earliest forms, but Hebrew has the distinction of having the above-mentioned layers attached to it, while Sanskrit is more vibration based. Hebrew is also more western world focused, while Sanskrit is still largely eastern world focused. This can be seen in the formulation of the letters. Sanskrit has aesthetic resemblances to the letters of other eastern languages, while Hebrew does not.

This brings us to an interesting point. There is more than one language family on the planet. For practical and basic purposes, let's look at the language family based on Latin (the Romance languages), and the language family containing Sanskrit (the Indo-Aryan), each of which fall within the larger Indo-European family. These language families all share traits in sound, grammar, and sentence structure, with more closely related languages being more similar. Comparing any of these to, for example, Chinese (a Sinitic language), the expectations that a native speaker of one of these languages has about how to construct words and sentences, or even how to write things down, simply don't work. I mention this here to let you, the reader, know that the study of languages has broken things down as scientifically as possible, and you may find it worthwhile to personally explore these codifications and classifications. The rest of the book will focus on what to do with language, but it is important to know the basic underpinnings of the modern approach to languages and language classifications.

Now on to the interesting crossroads this brings us to Hieroglyphics. While Hebrew was being developed in the Egyptian Empire for whatever reason, the most sacred and secret communication lines in Egypt were Hieroglyphics. Ancient Egyptians also had a spoken language, and a more common form of writing known as Demotic script, but still the Hieroglyphics, preserving an older form of language which was considered more holy and containing its religious and magical secrets, remained within the temples. The Rosetta Stone was the key to the deciphering of Hieroglyphics, but the interesting note on that is that it wasn't found until many centuries after the fall of the Egyptian empire. That means that when the Egyptian empire fell, most of its secrets were also lost. It has been rumored that there were Egyptian mystery tradition priests that kept the spoken language and the secret knowledge of how to read the texts of the Egyptians alive until approximately the fifth century CE, but when they died, so, too, did their knowledge. Truly, the Hieroglyphs were a source of awe for not only conquerors like Napoleon, but also all of the grave robbers that arrived before him and his subsequent "accidental" cosmetic surgery of the Sphinx, at least if that actually happened.

Suffice to say, here is the stance I will be taking in this book: Ancient Egyptians knew and understood the power of vibrations of letters and words upon their environment, and understood karmic law so well that they knew better than to develop a language in the same vein as their contemporaries, which at the time included the Hittites, Greeks, and to a lesser extent, the Phoenicians. My evidence for this theory is simple: Of the cultures I just mentioned, which ones made the biggest impact on the race of humanity? It could be argued that the Greeks made as big of an impact as the Egyptians, but the Greeks didn't begin their development as a culture until after the Egyptians had already been an empire for at least two thousand years[4]. The Greeks may have the ideas that led to the foundation of the Western World, but they learned what they knew from the same place the Twelve Tribes of Israel learned Hebrew, and whom the Hindus traded with: the Egyptians. Yes, my stance is simple: Every modern western magickal concept dates back to Ancient Egypt. But here's where it gets intense: Ancient Egypt dates back to Atlantis, and, before that, Lemuria, and even further back, Mu! Crazy, huh? Hope you're prepared for the ride....

---

[4] For more information, check out *The Mystery of the Sphinx* by Graham Hancock.

## Ancient and Modern Parallels

When deciding to cover the topic of language, I did have to define a starting point, which was a challenge. I went with the starting point of 50,000 years ago because I didn't think you, the reader, would be interested in exploring all the way back to the linguistic influence of Mu, and older. Another reason I chose this starting point was that it encompasses at least one ice age, and I believe that is very important when discussing modern civilization. As a whole, humanity dates back farther than 50,000 years, but we should keep this topic contemporary. A third reason that I chose that starting point is that it covers at least one zodiacal year, and close to a second as well, thus putting things into perspective from a skyward point of view. Language is a means of communicating, verbally, between at least two parties, and over the development of aeons, not only the mindset and thoughtforms of the two communicators have changed, but also the subject of said conversations. We'll talk about thoughtforms more in depth later on in this text. Around 26,000 BCE, many of the subjects that were being discussed verbally were a lot different than the ones being discussed today. For example, an overplayed but amusing representation of a conversation from 26,000 years ago would be something like this:

1) "Did you hear what the High Priest did today?"
2) "No, what did he do?"
1) "He didn't sacrifice a child. He sacrificed an elder!"
2) "What?!"
1) "It's true. I heard it from my brother, who was there. Guess that means drought. Guess that means tough times."
2) "Times have to be tough to do something that severe."

Today, it may go something like this:
1) "I got a text message from my frater today."
2) "Oh yeah? What did he have to say?"
1) I am late with my membership dues, and on Friday the Master of the Temple is going to call me to collect."
2) "Bummer, man. You got the cash?"
1) "Yep. Gonna make him call, though. Make him work for me like I work for him."
2) "Dude, you sure about that?"
1) "Yep."

There is a much different manner of speaking about spiritual issues today than there was that long ago. And there are a lot of ways that environmental factors are different from the ancient past. Each one of those factors, by the way, has become a setting for our spiritual development, so therefore they cannot be discounted in any way, shape, or form. However, due to these factors, language has become much more than it once was, while maintaining its core focus. It simply adapts to what we adapt to as an evolving species. This tells us that in the future language and the conveyance of ideas will change as we grow and evolve as a species. Here again the proof of this lies in the hieroglyphics that exist, for hieroglyphs are now considered outdated and antiquated, and have been replaced with other systems, while once they codified the ultimate in ancient sacred knowledge.

Some subjects haven't changed over the course of the last 50,000 years, though. As an ancient Hebrew philosopher once said, "there's nothing new under the sun." In a lot of ways, we as a society are dealing with the same things that we have always dealt with, and the only changes that are present are different faces and different environmental factors. Humanity will always deal with some common themes that have to do with the human condition. Themes such as corruption, power, kindness, compassion, and forgiveness will always be present for us. To compound this, it is also worth keeping in mind psychological archetypes, which is something that Dr Carl Jung went into extensive detail about in his life's work.

Without going into too much detail on archetypes, we can consider the fact that we now have two layers to communication: the archetypes, and, more consciously, a limited number of subjects that are usually discussed. Within these layers, though, there are almost endless combinations that can be had, and these combinations are as varied as the human race. This diversity means that as much as we learn about conscious control of language and thought, we can never know every detail and every situation that may come up. We can definitely learn the principles behind all of this so that we're almost never caught off guard. When this level of awareness is reached, we find ourselves more empowered than the average person who pays no heed to these ideas. A disclaimer from the book "Psychic Self-Defense" by Dion Fortune comes to mind here, which, paraphrased, states: "While my examples may become outdated, the principles are timeless." She was well aware that fashion and the use of language will change over time, but the principles that are addressed through these examples are eternal, and will always have relevance to people that populate society, especially when it comes to the western world.

As society becomes more and more global, we will come to a greater understanding of language and its application. We will remove the veil of ignorance that leaves us thinking that situations we face in our culture are not faced in other cultures. All cultures have very, very similar situations that they deal with, and while context may sometimes change, the underlying principles transcend cultural differences. Before the modern globalization, it was easy to think that what we were experiencing in the western world wasn't being experienced in eastern cultures, but this has been proven to be false. So many principles that we've been discussing are culture-less, and have to do with people rather than the global cultures that exist. In other words, language, communication, and the conveyance of ideas are all related to people, *not* to particular cultures. True, some cultures may have things occurring in them that are not occurring in other cultures, and these affect languages, but overall there are more common traits than there are differences. For example, corruption is corruption is corruption, regardless of where you are on the globe. The only thing that varies is what defines corruption. In one culture corruption may be simply not playing by the rules, while in another culture corruption may have to do with moral decisions that are not in line with the norm of society. When using language as a magical tool, context is one of the most if not the most important points to keep in mind. After all, when things are taken out of context, we move into the realms of misunderstanding and propaganda, and move away from the realm of objectivity and fact. When we do this, we remove ourselves from the common denominator that we all share, which is this consensual paradigm that we have all decided to inhabit at this time and in this fashion. While subjectivity is good in a lot of cases, it can be detrimental in just as many instances.

What I've attempted to do in this chapter is not only give you a very basic framework of the background and history of modern language, but also to give you a rough idea of some of the stances I'll be taking in later chapters. If the amount of information and the point of view it's taken from is too much for one digestion, feel free to pause in your study of this book and come back to it when you are ready. I also encourage you to do your own research on the roots of language so that you can decide for yourself what to believe, and what to discard. The focus of this book is not on an in depth history of language, but rather on what can be done with language from a magical perspective. Thus, what you believe when it comes to the history of language is ultimately irrelevant when put into context of what we'll be discussing here, but it is a fascinating body of work to study for individual growth and evolution. Controversy is just getting started, and while it may lead to enlightenment in the long run, losing interest in the short term is not my agenda. I'm here to expand minds and give food for thought, not insult and overwhelm. As long as you're focused on putting language to work for you as a magical tool, then the rest of this book will be a lot easier to digest than the historical and archaeological roots of language. Come on in, if you dare.

# Chapter 2
# The Interconnectedness of
# Language and Culture

In the previous chapter we discussed, albeit briefly, the history of language. This chapter will be a brief overview of the inter-relatedness of language and culture, and thus will be an extension of something that we touched on previously. It is important to realize how the two affect each other, and the symbiotic relationship they enjoy. Many sociological texts have been written for the halls of academia on this subject, and for further study I would recommend contacting your favorite educational institution for recommendations. I will simply be addressing the barest of bones in this text.

If you have one physical being, you can still have outward vibratory communication because there are at least two listeners[5], but only one of the entities is producing corporeal sound and actual vibrations in the air. However, when you have two physical beings engaging in a discussion, things change. Both can have outward vibrations, and both can hear the vibrations of the other. More importantly, both have their own interpretation of what the other is vibrating. Immediately this propels us into a new realm: physical vibratory initiation and physical vibratory reception.

It is important to explain here the above use of vibrate as opposed to communicate or language, or derivatives thereof. Vibrate, as we will cover in the next chapter, is what we are essentially doing whenever we use our voice box to communicate. It is vibrations that are

---

[5] I refer here to such discarnate beings as spirit guides and non-physical entities.

issued forth from our mouth when we communicate vocally. Vibrations are also involved with visual communication, whether art or sign language, encode our radio and television signals, and drive our technology. Basic science has covered this, so I see no reason to go over that same ground here, but it is wise to remember this basic physical fact.

The concept of vibrating words is something that is an integral part of the Western Esoteric Tradition. It is worth detailing out vibrations in the name of clarity. There are many different forms of vibration, and technically everything is vibrating. However, what differs from item to item and subject to subject is how much something is vibrating. For example, steel is vibrating at a much, much slower rate than plastic. It is then obvious that a lot of this has to do with the density of matter, but that is a subject for another time. When this principle is extrapolated, it becomes clear that even things that may seem abstract, such as light, are also vibrating.

Visual vibration is something that we should be aware of as well. There are two parts of vibrations that are worth being aware of. The first part refers to the things that we can see and touch that are vibrating, such as the examples listed above. However, the other part of vibrations has to do with the things that vibrate that we don't consciously recognize. These are vibrations that occur outside the realm of the five senses, even at the atomic level. However, they are vibrating nonetheless, and having an impact on us, even though we may not be consciously aware of them. Thus, at this point in the text, I choose to refer to it as "vibrations" as opposed to "communication" for these reasons, but I will change to communication, communicate, and other derivatives, after crossing into section two of this text. Anyway, back to the point.

## Physical Group Vibrations

Physical group vibrations occur when there are two or more physical beings engaging in an exchange of ideas. Most commonly this is known as a discussion, but it can also be two beings humming, chanting, panting, or otherwise producing sound to express ideas, emotions, concepts, or experiences. In any event, there are two factors present. One being is the initiator, vibrating and sending out audio waves to an audience. The other being, or beings, is the receiver, receiving the vibrated audio waves being sent out by the first party, and interpreting those waves in a fashion that they find personally comprehensible. In a group setting, when the above criteria are met, you have some concept being transmitted, and that concept is of utmost importance. If someone vibrates to you that the sky is blue, do you understand that they are conveying to you their concept of the appearance of the sky? Or do you pass a judgment on that individual for saying something that you believe to be not only common sense, but also so common that it doesn't merit a passing thought? When someone tells me the sky is blue, my immediate response is to ask him or her: "What makes you say that?" By questioning the initiator, in effect, the receiver (or receivers) is attempting to understand the point of reference from which the initiator speaks. This in turn sends a very powerful vibratory message to the initiator. That message is similar to this: "What I perceive is that what you 'tell' me is that you believe the sky is blue. However, I must know that I am understanding you correctly when I deduce that." In communication and writing circles, this is known as the Rogerian communication strategy. Some say this necessarily emerges from an assumption that there is already a communication breakdown. However, it is this author's opinion that it is better to prevent than to deal with it on the back end. In my opinion, proactivity is always better than reactivity.

This can have a very big impact on the rest of the thought form and energetics of future messages transmitted from that particular initiator to that particular receiver or receivers. If it is taken for granted that the initiator merely means that the sky is blue in their eyes, it may also mean that when the initiator says, "god is dead", the receiver believes that the initiator is referring to a common god form, and not necessarily the godform of the receiver or receivers, or even the godform of the initiator! This in turn produces a perceived division between initiator and receiver, and perceived division is generally not good.

A way around such perceived division is establishing that the initiator and receiver have the same concept of god (using the above example). While this is normally assumed as a consequence of the attraction of like minds, it can never be taken for granted. As soon as it is taken for granted, a doorway is opened that could lead to a communication breakdown, which generally does more harm than good. For example, I have many friends that I have known for years and when they tell me something they believe to be true about god, I must make sure I know what they mean. Even though we have similar concepts of the godform and godhead, I have never walked a mile in their shoes, so I cannot be sure as to what they are referring. Therefore I will ask them something akin to: "Your god is dead?" Or "Are you talking about your belief in the godhead?" This generally clarifies things enough to proceed with the vibratory exchange.

The impact of thoughtforms and energetics on future transmissions from initiator to receiver or receivers can be almost apocalyptic. This is the true root of double talk that appears in many media messages, in everything from Hollywood productions to the political arena. For example, the entire plot of a movie could be rooted in the antagonist saying that he or she would release the hostages after the protagonist met the antagonist's demands, but after the demands are met, the antagonist declares, "I didn't say when". Not only does this portray that character as despicable, but it also drives home something taken for granted in today's world. If we as the human race want to progress as far as we can, we should be as exact as possible in our speech and vibratory exchanges to keep such above fictitious scenarios from happening. To put it simply, there is power in a question, and that power should be exercised by all; for the ability to question has been given to all that read this. The intent and meaning of a message should never be assumed if there is any doubt or ambiguity. Always question until comfortable!

For those of you that are not familiar with thoughtforms, let me take a moment to explain them. The term thoughtform comes from Theosophy, and is quite a potent idea which can be very powerful to work with. In essence, it is an extrapolation from the idea that thoughts have energy, and that repetitive patterns of thought can generate particular patterns and effects. This can even be taken to suggest that these patterns and forms may even develop consciousness over time, and thus can act of their own accord. A prime example of this is an addiction. When someone does their best to break a particular addiction, they are in essence pitting their will against the will of the thoughtform that has been created through the repeated use of the tool of their addiction. The thoughtform that goes along with the addiction has achieved consciousness, and doesn't want to go away. As an extension of this, it is also common that the energy behind the addiction transfers to a new addiction in order to continue its existence. I realize that this is a brief and broad definition of a thoughtform, but it is necessary so that we are all on the same page and can move forward with a shared basis for understanding.

## Physical Group Vibratory Reception

Physical group vibratory reception is the next step in the analysis. As will be shown in the next chapter, it is simply an interpretation of what we receive through our eardrums. This is paramount because we as a species have common racial[6] ideas and teachings. For example, if I vibrate the word "tree", both you the receiver, and I the initiator, know approximately what that means. There is, of course, variance within that concept, but we have a common understanding of what a tree is. Ergo it stands to reason that I can communicate the word "tree" safely, with very little possibility of being misunderstood. This is not always true with other words, and especially not true when discussing topics such as magick and personal paradigms. Besides the above example of "god", if I were to vibrate to you the word "lust", how would you interpret it? Going by the dictionary and common known usage of the word, you would most likely think something akin to desire. However, in this case, you would be mistaken, for I mean it in the very Thelemic way of "The enjoyment of the exercising of strength.[7]

After such a common word is examined, is it now clear where miscommunication comes from, and why this book is necessary? To communicate clearly with your audience you must first know your audience. Advertising executives have understood this principle for years, and I am simply applying it to a magickal end. If one is not the initiator, one is the receiver. Yes, one can be both, but

---

[6] When I say racial here, I do not mean black, white, etc. I simply mean that we, as a race, have common beliefs.

[7] *The Book of Thoth*, Aleister Crowley, Weiser Publications, reprinted 1998.

communication does proceed in turns, and any given component of it is directional.

Advertisers have again grasped another facet of these vibrations: the idea of the subliminal message. We all know that messages can be put in between the lines of communication, as it were, and that our color of outfit as well as hand gestures can influence the tone and message of the exchange. Related to this is subconscious behavior. This includes those things that occur that are not consciously attracting our attention. This does slightly tie into subliminal thought and behavior, and because of this, the two can be studied together. Not everyone is aware of their subconscious behavior, while others use subtle and subconscious behavior to their advantage. I do encourage you to explore the use of the subconscious with regards to personal development and magick in general.

Physical group vibratory reception is an art in and of itself, much like physical vibratory initiation is an art. In other words, there is art in being a listener as well as a talker. While this is a commonly known fact for most, it needs to be taken here with a little more attention. We deal in the realms that affect not only the physical world around us, but also the other side of the veil. Therefore, we should be as precise as possible in all manners of communication so that we don't manifest something we didn't ask for or attract unwanted attention from undesirable entities. When we listen we are not only thinking with our brain, but we are also receiving energetic impressions on an empathic level. You don't have to be an empath to receive these energetics, but being an empath gives you a certain heightened sense about them that others don't have. Simply being aware that the energetics exist can give surprising control over them and their influence upon you.

If an idea is received by one being, it now has power. If more than one being receives the same idea and processes it similarly, the power of said idea thus increases accordingly. This is known as "exponential amplification," and basically says that the more people engage in an activity that is focused around energy, the greater the effect of manifestation. I mention this now as insight into the idea of a thoughtform, and to stress how important it is to be precise in both speech and understanding of ideas. For example, if you as the initiator vibrate the word "tree", as in the previous example, and I receive it to mean a tree you would find in a forest, then there is power there. However, if my friend that stands next to me hears you vibrate that same string of syllables, and immediately thinks of the Qabalah, the tree of life, then part of the initiator's message is lost. There is already a miscommunication, and there are only three people involved in the conversation! A perfect example of this is that phrase "tree of life", because it differs from culture to culture. In some cultures, this concept has to do with a central world tree that is central to life, whereas, as mentioned above, it can also represent the Qabala, or the mythological tree in the book of Genesis. Imagine the issues involved with authors of books and teachers of classes! Almost overwhelming, huh?

Non-physical group communication is only going to be mentioned in passing here. If you have two beings of a non-physical nature communicating, the vibratory wavelength they are working on is generally of a higher pitch frequency than we as humans can relate to, or that we are even able to physically receive. The focus of this text is on what we as physical humans can apply to our lives and our spiritual development. Later on in this book we will address a physical being interacting with a non-physical being, but not two nonphysical entities communicating.

Now we move on to cultural aspects of vibratory communication. As mentioned earlier, beings tend to gravitate to those of like minds. There are many reasons why this is, and most good psychology texts will address this issue in depth. I will simply focus on an overview of such behaviors. Not only are we talking about cultures based on geographical and political boundaries, we are also talking about cultures that are based more along the lines of shared beliefs. Yes, the technical term for this is subculture, but to the people involved in it, it is generally experienced as a standard culture rather than a subculture. For example, consider your local spiritual belief community. If it is not in line with the dominant belief system of the society you find yourself in, then technically it would be considered a subculture of said society. However, does that really matter to you? To most people it doesn't matter, for it is *their* culture, and that is first and foremost. This is the point that I will be working from for a large part of this text.

As beings in physical form, we tend to gravitate to those that share our worldview. Our reasons are generally rooted in such psychological factors as looking for acceptance, discussion of common ideas, and mental and spiritual growth. Over time, culture will develop out of this group "mind" and habits will form that will set this culture apart from others. These habits can be physical things like styles of clothing and self-expression, or it can be more cerebral things such as speech patterns and common terms used in language. In any event, what defines a culture can also be an albatross. An outsider will, as a culture becomes better-known and better-codified, almost always be able to spot a member, whether by appearance or behavior or both. It is possible to blend in with other cultures outside of one's own. However, in so doing, a certain duality is invoked, and unless this duality is under firm control, problems of hypocrisy and internal division can arise. See, for example, the Kurt Vonnegut Jr. novel "Mother Night" for further elucidation. There are also a number of studies and explorations of what is called "code-switching", which is modulating between several language variations in order to move more smoothly or safely in different cultures, which you may be interested in exploring.

An interesting point to mention here is the concept of slang. Often times a word means something different in a particular culture than its meaning in a different one. To the outsider this can be a difficult idea to navigate, as it creates the potential for communication rupture, but if you're in the culture, this is easy to understand. Earlier I mentioned Aleister Crowley's use of the word "lust," and now I'll give another example: the word "religion." In Spiritualism, religion simply means "living in harmony with natural and universal laws," but I believe that we are all familiar with a different definition of religion that is commonly used by society. Hence it is always wise to get clarification on words that may seem like they're used out of context when used in a subculture group. Perhaps they're not used out of context, but rather they have a different meaning than what we're used to.

Part of this seeking lies in a sort of spiritual longing to connect with those of a similar vibration. As certain schools of metaphysics teach us, on the other side of the veil souls spend time with those of a similar vibration. This is why a physically manifested incarnation is so valuable: it allows us to interact with those that have vibrations that are different from our own, and thus a soul can work through karma in a faster fashion than it can on the other side of the veil. Thus the soul intuitively desires to be with those that have a similar vibration to it while in physical form, and to avoid those who have a vibration that is not in tune with their own. Whether the individual is aware of this metaphysical teaching is irrelevant; the manifestation of this quest still occupies the bulk of a lifetime. Think of it this way: When we connect with people of a similar vibration, we tend to feel like we are home and welcome. This is a truism that exists whether one is aware of esoteric explanations or not, much like blood circulates through the body regardless of whether or not the person is aware of the science behind the blood flow.

Can there be a culture without the use of language? Is it possible to gravitate to those of like mind if no outward vibratory exchange happens? It is my belief that this is not a possibility within the current state of evolution of humanity and, in particular, western world society. However, it is still possible that there are some groups of people out there that could operate this way. What is it that draws a culture into being? It is an audio exchange of vibrations that are in synchronicity with each other, and if there is no exchange, then that aspect of reality never comes into being. The only exception to this is that of an individual's work with spirit guides and beings on the other side of the veil. For example, if I do extensive work with a spirit guide by the name of "Hal", and he leads me to meet you, who also works extensively with a spirit guide named "Hal", then in the broadest definition of culture, we have just formed one, and, quite possibly, no audio vibratory exchange has happened. It has just been two spirit guides, or one guide acting on two fronts, that has prompted this meeting of minds.

What are the strengths found in belonging to a culture? The predominant one, from an energetic standpoint, is that the more people that work with a certain current of energy, and certain thoughtforms associated therewith, the more energy that current receives and has at its disposal. Remember the exponential increase of energy from people invested in the same project? Take, for example, some of the godforms that are in use today. Isis is a much more common deity than Tiamat, so therefore energy associated with her is simply more potent than what is associated with Tiamat[8], and this translates to more energetic weight behind Isis than Tiamat. Both ideas are powerful and profound to work with, but we're talking about raw energy here, not the deities themselves. However, the converse can be quite effective as well. For example, if you were seeking a goddess that stood out, and that would see you as more unique, then Tiamat might be the way to go. Isis would still see you as unique, of course, but you would be of a smaller number following Tiamat, which has its own form of power.

Yes, I am going out on a limb here and claiming something that isn't addressed a lot. There is something to be said for the amount of followers on any given spiritual path. In essence, the more followers, the stronger the current of energy available for manipulation. Yes, this is a modern spirituality text, and I used the word "manipulation" freely. Why? That is what all of us are doing every time we do any form of magick. It's how we go about said manipulation and the intention behind it that places each of us into our own comfortable cultures. Within said cultures, we fine-tune manipulating the energetics associated with the current of energy we are working with. If you belong to a culture that supplicates and you then enter a culture where that is not the way, you would be thrown off kilter, and may even feel uncomfortable or dis-empowered. Over time this awkwardness would dissipate, but initially it can cause discomfort.

What do the above observations have to do with culture and language? Being a member of a culture has a certain impact on not only your surroundings, but also your magickal work. If reality is language, and language defines culture, then it is of utmost importance to be careful what you say, because you may draw to you a

---

[8] I would like to insert here that I am NOT passing any judgment here one-way or the other. I'm simply illustrating a point.

culture that does not fit, or that will covertly lead you astray from your spiritual path. Secondly, when involved in a culture, you can control the energetics of said culture by simply using the right words in the right context with the right definitions, and knowing the right questions to ask, and when. Third, remember context and mental clarity. If you are a member of a culture that works with a deity that is not widely known, then manifestations from magical workings with that deity may not appear to the same magnitude as they might if you worked with a deity who has contributions from a larger number of people. The manifestations and results may still come, but they may take more effort to achieve, or may simply manifest in a way that is different than the norm.

To sum all of this technical jargon up simply:

1) Know what you say when you say it.

2) Know that you hear correctly what is meant to be heard by the initiator.

3) If you aren't sure about something, ask the right questions for clarifications.

4) Be aware that your audience may not always be in physical form. By following these suggestions, you can accomplish greater control over your life and what vibrates to you. You can also achieve greater clarity on the mental plane, which means that you open yourself up to higher vibrations and greater empowerment.

How will you know the right questions to ask? Listen to your intuition and your guides. Your guides are on your side and want to help you evolve. If you feel one of them is leading you astray, it would be wise to reassess your workings and your relationship with them. If spirit guides are not in your paradigm, then your intuition is your best friend. After all, it comes from within you, and has no beginning outside of you, so it can be trusted, at least as long as you can trust yourself. You can use it to cultivate this relationship by trusting yourself in small ways, eventually building on those successes and leading up to bigger ways. For example, if your intuition is saying to take a different route to work and that route wouldn't add much more time to your commute, then take that route. Usually there is a reason for this that becomes apparent after you have arrived at your destination. It could be that you avoided an accident, or perhaps you avoided road construction. You may even simply benefit from the change in scenery, get a nice view, or energize yourself by allowing yourself more flexibility for your day. Whatever the case may be, you discover you saved yourself a headache.

A more verbal technique that can be used similarly involves listening to the "voice inside your head" when you are engaged in conversation with someone. By listening to that voice when it says to say something or withhold something, you begin to trust yourself more when interacting with people. The trick to success is to go with the intuition rather than attempting to analyze why you feel this is best and appropriate. You may also find that it is wise to research the subject of the vibratory exchange that is occurring. The topic of research isn't emphasized enough from my perspective. By thoroughly researching and understanding what it is that we want to know more about, we can then ask more educated questions. Many people are simply content *not* to research a given topic, and then wonder why the topic is different in practice than it is in theory. Research promotes critical thinking skills, and critical thinking skills promote a healthier and more empowered type of spiritual development. The more we know about the focus of our spiritual path, the better position we are in to achieve rapid spiritual growth, and the more of a position we are in to receive more information from non-physical beings that exist to assist us.

Keep journalistic ideas in mind if you're not sure of a message being conveyed: who, what, where, why, when, and how are six of the most potent questions you can employ in your day to day life. They are just as important when it comes to translating messages that are coming to us, whether those messages originate from a physical source or not. Every subject that you hear spoken of can be addressed and refined with a selection of these six questions, and because of this, you have the ability to take it apart piece by piece in the name of greater understanding. I do realize that at most times things are accepted verbatim, but there are times when our intuition guides us to inquire further, and when we do, we may discover information that was kept from us, or information that matters to us that didn't matter to other people. Our intuition is the knife's edge, so to speak, and by using it wisely and cautiously, we can focus on the things that matter, rather than the superfluous.

All six questions that are mentioned above also help to promote greater objectivity when it comes to assessing the information we receive. Too frequently subjectivity is highlighted with regards to spiritual growth, but objectivity is something that deserves much more emphasis than it receives. Objectivity promotes detachment, and detachment promotes good emotional health. By looking at a subject from multiple perspectives, we open ourselves up to perspectives that are not ours, but may still have validity. If we look at things objectively, we can then speak in a clearer way that can be understood by a greater number of people, while if we limit ourselves to subjectivity and closed mindedness our vocal magick is constrained by our own intimate and unique perspective. It is one thing to convey an idea from our point of view, but it is a much more powerful technique if we convey an idea from our point of view, and then discuss alternate viewpoints and perspectives and relate them together. This also helps to avoid conflict by drawing in a variety of perspectives, and in this way our commitment to objectivity helps keep the peace, as it were, between parties that may have different subjective views, yet have a common ultimate goal.

As a matter of fact, looking at things objectively and letting the facts speak for themselves are two of the hallmarks of the scientific method. When scientific method thinking is employed often enough, it will bleed over into speech and communication. This is a wonderful tool for seeing things as they are, rather than how we want to see them. This is important because only through seeing things as they are can we make more accurate, clearer, and informed decisions. This can propel us forward on our spiritual path faster than if we didn't employ these techniques. Using the scientific method of thinking and ultimately speaking can make our intent clearer and more conducive to discussion. Thus arguments are avoided, and impassioned perspectives can still be honored. All of this focus on the mental plane is important because the mental plane is higher than the emotional plane, which is higher than the physical plane. The order of the planes will be mentioned and discussed throughout this book, but for now it is enough to know that by looking at things objectively, we intentionally raise our vibration so that higher vibrational beings resonate with us, and thus we open ourselves to greater amounts of wisdom.

In short, energy flows where thoughts go, and thought begets form. Thus, when we realize that we have an audience, and that we play the role of both projector and receptor, we acknowledge the complexity that is associated with communication in all of its forms. At the root of communication is vibration, and these vibrations can be altered and controlled at will if one is conscious of this metaphysical science. The key to unlocking all of this potential is to be objective, and in order to be objective, we must first practice objectivity in the comfort of our own mind so that it becomes second nature. When it becomes second nature to be objective in thought, we then find that it becomes much easier to be objective in speech, regardless of whether this is a conscious or subconscious act. It is better for this to be a conscious choice so that we can have control over it, but often it is something that occurs subconsciously, and we recognize this behavior within ourselves only after we recognize that people are interacting with us differently than they had before. Sometimes we recognize this shift in our energy field by noticing that certain people are no longer present in our lives as much as they used to be. Other times we discover this shift in our energy field by noting that new people are coming into our lives more and more frequently, and we pause to ask ourselves "Why?" Thus, we find ourselves coming full circle to the philosopher's question where we began our explorations. I always find it interesting when synchronicities like this happen, for it lets us know that we are on the right track with our spiritual and magical growth.

# Chapter 3
## The Physiology Behind the Art

This chapter will be the last of the technical talk that is necessary in order to set the stage for what comes next. I will be covering the science of speech, vibrations, and how we actually vibrate what comes across as language and communication. I will also discuss the science behind hearing and briefly cover how important it is to know your own body. It is too easy in today's society of convenience and disposability to take speech (and, to a greater extent, the human body) for granted. The human body that each of us has is a wonderful and beautiful machine, capable of many amazing things. Any body has capacities that a non-corporeal entity cannot experience, as our True Self knows when it chooses an embodiment, including its faults, which may be reflections of particular challenges or resolutions to karmic issues.

Of all the physical challenges there are in the world, those affecting the voice are in the minority. Most affect either the limbs or different systems within the body. Yes, there are those afflictions that affect the speech and vocalization processes, but by and large they are in the minority. This means that of all the challenges we as incarnated beings may face at the behest of our True Selves, or as consequences for previous actions of our will choice, vocalization is one of the most stalwart and dependable systems of the body. Here's the question, though: Do we treat this gift as it deserves, or do we take it for granted? I would guess that most of us lie somewhere in the middle and for the most part appreciate it, but sometimes lapse into taking it for granted. There's nothing wrong with that-we're in physical form, so we're not perfect. I simply pose the question to stimulate gratitude and thought. By asking why we do things, we spur our spiritual growth forward just a little bit faster. Through questioning our own motives, we begin to gain greater control over our actions, and thus our impact upon the world, including how we are perceived in general.

The process of vocalization has a huge impact. Not only does it affect our spiritual growth but it also plays a major hand in our interaction with the world of illusion that we all interact with to some extent every day. How easy would it be to go through our daily routine if we could not speak? A Tibetan technique that a friend of mine told me about some time ago bears mentioning, even though its focus is for more esoteric purposes than I cite here. Try this and see how you do: Try going a day not speaking a word. If you are in a relationship similar to a marriage where that would actually cause more problems than benefits, tell your partner what you are doing, and then speak as little as possible to them during the course of the day. See how communication becomes difficult? I won't discuss the rest of what that test may say, but consider it a learning experience. We live in the Western World, and speech is necessary for us to get by. Therefore, it stands to reason that taking care of our vocal system should be one of our top priorities. However, part of the esoteric lesson of this technique is that there is great wisdom and value in silence, almost as much value as there is in speech. Sometimes it's the pauses in conversation that reveal more than the actual conversation themselves.

## Speech

The science of speech, in a nutshell, is simple. When we choose to speak, our breath travels up from our lungs and diaphragm and interacts with our vocal cords. Depending on the person, it may not be a conscious choice to control such a function. Once that exhaled air reaches our vocal cords at the base of the larynx it vibrates against them, and depending on how tight they are determines the pitch they resonate[9]. Of course we control how tight the vocal cords are; therefore we control the pitch we resonate. Conversely, it would stand to reason that there is a limit to that control, much as there is a limit to our capacity with our other muscles. Since we have limits as human beings, we are limited in what we can vibrate. Let's revisit the previous example of the hearing of a dog. A dog whistle can reach a higher vibration than we can produce in our throats, and higher than most of us can perceive with our ears, which is why it has a different impact on a dog than if we were to just whistle. Humans cannot hear every sound that is out there, much like every other animal on the planet. Every animal is limited to what it can hear by a variety of physical factors. Arguably, there is more that we can't hear than what we *can* hear. This concept has been addressed in many different ways in society throughout the years. A common urban legend reminds us that often times malls play music that has subliminal messages during the holiday season to encourage consumers to buy more. While there have been many laws put in place regarding subliminal advertising, it does still occur in one way or another.

Another limitation of the pitch we issue forth has to do with not only where we are on our spiritual path, but also our environmental upbringing. For example, as well documented in the book *Power vs. Force*[10], our environmental upbringing plays a huge role in our vibrations, as well as how far we can progress in the realm of spiritual development. It takes a great amount of courage to take steps to rise above our upbringing, but when this is accomplished, we can move into whatever

[9] *The Human Body*, Charles Clayman MD-Editor in Chief; Dorling Kindersley Limited; London, 1995.
[10] *Power vs. Force*; David R. Hawkins M.D., Ph.D.; Hay House, Inc.; reprinted 2002.

position that we choose to in society. The trick to this is in learning what it is that we need to learn to increase our station to produce a higher quality life for ourselves. This also means that there can be a created limit to what we can vibrate through our throats.

If, for example, you had a very high pitched voice as a child that (surprisingly) stayed with you through puberty, but were surrounded by family members who thought this was not normal, it would at least subconsciously limit how far you developed it into adulthood. Such non-desired restrictions would have at least a subconscious impact on your development, likely making you less willing to use the power of your voice to affect the world. The easiest way to explain it is in terms of classical conditioning from psychology. The more we are told we can or can't do something, the more we believe it. This limits how far we can go on our spiritual path this incarnation, but that doesn't stop the True Self's growth over many incarnations, nor should we pass any judgment on the ego self because of it.

Everything is karmic. If there is a reason that we can't vibrate the pitch that we want in our throat, there's a reason for it. Even if we as our ego selves don't know what that reason is, there is one. We may not know what it is until after the change called death, but nonetheless it exists. Does that mean that we should just accept it? No, not at all. By striving to raise our vibrations in speech and inflections in communication, we are also raising our vibration overall, and that is a conceptually good thing. The higher the vibration, the closer to godhead we become. The more we can influence change in our surroundings and ourselves, and the better we can manifest our goals. In effect, we move into an increasingly close rhythm with ascension energies.

Why is raising our pitch in speech a good thing? Quite simply, it gives us finer control over our vocal cords, and thereby greater control over our physical form. By gaining better control over our physical form, we are gaining better control over ourselves. By gaining better control over ourselves, we are fulfilling the old oracle lesson of "Know thyself". By fulfilling this lesson, we are gaining a finer control over our finer bodies. By gaining a finer control over our finer bodies, we are having a much greater impact on our environment. Oh, my kingdom for a nail[11]!

It has also been noted that there are positive psychological effects that are brought about by singing, so it is wise to indulge in that as well as other things that bring joy to our lives. Succinctly, singing reduces stress, and thus we live a more relaxed life.

To manifest in a more positive way is also to be very aware of what you say when you speak, but I will not cover that here. I will give much attention to that topic in the next part of this book. Suffice to say that words that have a more positive meaning correlate to words that are higher in pitch, and words that have a more negative meaning correlate to words that are said with a lower pitch. Thus, one can see how this affects manifestation, or the lack thereof.

How do we take care of our throats to ensure that we can speak within the full range of what we as humans are capable of? First it should be understood that not all people have the same range. The clearest example of this that comes to mind is popular singers. Mariah Carey has a greater range than, say, the lead singer of the average heavy metal band. This illustrates that not all of us have the same range, and, as stated before, this is most likely karmic in origin. But, we can still do the best with what we have by following basic tenets of care. First, things that harm the throat should be avoided, or in some circumstances, handled in moderation. Smoking is harsh

---

[11] This is taken from the nursery rhyme: For Want of a Nail.

on the throat. Lemon juice is good for the throat. Any good vocal instructor or books on the voice can yield a variety of tips and techniques that will help. Even a simple search on the Internet could yield useful results. Yes, all of this may seem like a lot of work, but in this author's opinion, the development of your spiritual path is worth this amount of work and so much more. Self care is something that cannot be stressed enough, but this goes beyond the basic tenets of healthy boundaries, etc. Self care also covers the physical side of life, and sometimes it takes getting an education to know what to use to take care of what part of the body.

Speech and the vocal cords are some of the easiest things we can control on our spiritual path. We must never forget that, and we must always be aware of the potency given to us through this simple process. If we do misstep, there are plenty of non-physical beings that would love to help us with learning this lesson. Don't believe me? Try it. Say something you believe to be true, and then watch the lesson it brings play out. As soon as we profess something to be true, then we are tested on it by the universe. If we are aware of this karmic law, then we can remain open to receiving wisdom rather than feeling like our viewpoint is being challenged for no reason. Controlling our speech is one of the easiest things we can do to change our world, but in order to do this, we must first change our thoughts and remain conscious of our speech, even when our emotions are intense.

### Hearing

In essence, as with speech, the science behind hearing is very simple. Sound vibrations are channeled through the ear canal and vibrate against the eardrum. The eardrum then transmits those vibrations via nerves to the brain. The brain, in turn, translates said vibrations into what we understand as speech and language, thus originating communication. This is why I didn't use the word (or its derivatives) communication in the first two chapters. We must not forget that when someone initiates communication with us, they are simply sending out vibrations. What we perceive as speech isn't a reality. Our brain makes it a reality. The essence is vibrations sent out by an initiator. Why do I go to the trouble of explaining it in such detail? Why is such detail important? Those answers will come in part two of this book.

With regards to hearing, it is a very simple process. First, the receiver takes in the vibrations that the initiator sends out. If there is a defective eardrum, then the process stops there. If the eardrum is in at least partial working order, the process continues. If the eardrum is only in partial working order, the vibrations from the initiator are received, but not relayed to the brain in their full context. There is still a partial message received, but it is not the full message because the eardrum isn't translating the vibrations the way it would in normal function. Thus we have the first possible problem in communication. The receiver may not be physically able to receive the vibrations being sent out from the initiator. This is something that is out of the control of not only the initiator, but also of the receiver. For whatever reason, the eardrum doesn't function as it should, and therefore part of the vibratory message is lost in translation to the receiver's brain.

After the vibrations are received via the ear canal and eardrum, the vibrations are sent to the brain via nerves. Here, there could be another physical limitation that inhibits the intended message of the initiator. If the eardrum works fine, but the nerves are damaged (for whatever reason), the message would not be translated correctly in the brain of the recipient or recipients. This would prevent clear communication from happening, and thus conveying the message would be a failure. However, if the nerves are in complete working order, the vibrations are sent to the brain in the manner intended by the initiator (for the most part. There are empathic problems that the initiator may encounter, but we will discuss those later), and thus are translated correctly in the brain of the receiver (or receivers).

If the initiator lacks the ability to convey a message clearly, from a physical sense, that will create additional challenges. For example, if the initiator has a tongue that doesn't work right, they may be unable to convey clearly the message they choose. There may also be challenges with their voice box and vocal cords, which may impede clear communication. One may simply not be able to speak what is on their mind clearly, and because of this, they may get frustrated, which can impede future exchange attempts.

This leads us to the next step of the process. When the brain receives the translation from the nerves, it interprets said vibratory translations according to its best principles and established tools. For example, if the receiver has never been exposed to the concept of an Ibis in any way, shape, or form, when you describe an Ibis, it will be lost on the receiver, and this is not the receiver's fault. The initiator would need a picture and a description that the receiver could relate to in order for this communication to be successful. The brain has limitations, as does any other part of the body, and the brain will only work within said confines. For example, if the receiver has always lived in an urban setting and never had any exposure to life on a farm, they would not be able to immediately understand the processes behind rotation planting or the reason behind skinning a buck immediately after hunting. But, the brain would be well equipped to understand metaphors that apply to an urban lifestyle. It must never be forgotten that being the initiator of a message is only half of the equation. There is also a receiver part, and that cannot be taken for granted. Each one of us, every day, is a receiver and an initiator of communication. Therefore we must always remain vigilant regarding what we say, and how we process what is conveyed to us. We are only in nearly full control of what we send out. We control how we process what we receive (to a certain degree), so we need to never neglect our duties as human beings.

In essence, the message intended by the initiator needs to be conveyed in a manner best suited for the audience. This sounds elementary, I know. But, how many times have you delivered a message that you thought was understood clearly, only to discover later, much to your chagrin, that it was misinterpreted? The astrological complications will be discussed later, but in the grand scheme of things, those complications cannot be a catchall excuse for problems. We as initiators must take responsibility for our words and be more cognizant of what we say, when we say it, and how we say it. We, as receivers, must be more willing to ask questions of our initiators to understand what it is they are trying to convey. I'm a big fan of asking questions if one is unclear. As a matter of fact, my curious nature has cost me a lot in this lifetime. There have been too many times that questions have not been asked, and that deficiency has led to a loss of clarity when it comes to the message being conveyed. There can be no taking for granted such a common and necessary facet of our lives. The better we deal with communication from our fellow human beings, the better we can deal with communication from Spirit and those beyond the veil. The better we deal with communication from Spirit, the more we will receive from Spirit, as long as we are upholding our end of the deal by sharing what we should. The more this relationship is cultivated, the more effective blending can occur, making the nonphysical physical.

Every day we go through this process multiple times and are barely aware of the principles behind it. We are always communicating on so many levels that sometimes we are overwhelmed on a subconscious level and that disempowers us. While it is okay for us to feel that, we cannot use that as a shield or an excuse for escaping personal responsibility. The average person in the western world is exposed to more information than any person at any given time in history, especially if computers are involved, and because of this, we find that our discernment skills should be more finely tuned than generations before us. This freedom of communication also makes it easier to achieve greater spiritual growth in a shorter amount of time.

By understanding the science behind speech and hearing, we can gain better control over ourselves and, ultimately, our universe. These previous three chapters are just to set the stage for what is to come in part two of this book. In part two, we will be discussing more magickal applications such as thought forms, karmic law, and what exactly vibrations do on a tangible level. I hope that I have conveyed clearly how the process of speech and hearing works in a clearly understood scientific fashion, without getting too technical or verbose. It is necessary to know how the physical side of things is arranged so that when we discuss the non-physical side of thing, it can all be brought back to the very clear and simple science of it all.

## Mudras

*Mudras* are hand gestures that are used extensively in Hinduism and Buddhism, but have found their way to the western world over the last several decades. There are more to mudras than just hand gestures, but for the sake of this treatise, I will only focus on the hands. There are mudras that are a combination of the hand and other limbs and poses of the body, but that is a topic for another time. As can be deduced, mudras involve bending and folding the fingers and hands, either individually or together, to tap into a certain kind of energy. Hence you have mudras for deities and specific goals, and sometimes both. I have always found mudras to be very subtle and useful due to the fact that they can be done easily, and generally without people seeing you do them, since the hand is faster than the eye. In situations where subtlety is the best way to react, these can be just what the doctor ordered.

If you are familiar with palmistry, then mudras will make a lot of sense to you. If you're not, I suggest that you do become familiar with it so you can place these techniques in greater context. Palmistry is useful because it can provide you with the knowledge that will let you compose your own mudras based on the planetary correspondences for fingers and different parts of the hand. In some ways, mudras are types of sigils because they operate on those they are affecting on a subconscious level. Hence, if you work with a certain deity and they have a mudra, you can use the mudra to tap into their energy, and this will affect the other person or people in the conversation.

Let us layer this idea, though. We can use mudras while we speak so that what we are saying and the mudra itself amplify and reinforce each other. I've found that a good way to approach this uses the mudra as a type of exclamation point. Hence I'll use mudras after speaking about something to cause greater effect. I'll use them in a very subtle way, generally where they can't be seen, and it's like closing out the statement. If you're familiar with the Qabala, it's like the final "Heh" in "Yod Heh Vau Heh." There are other techniques that have come to popularity in the United States that use mudra type gestures as well. If you're familiar with NLP, you can see many parallels with mudras. NLP, or Neuro-linguistic programming, is a current trend, and it has to do with verbal and physical interactions to program situations. So, in other words, it's a type of hypnosis with a more physically active flare to it. We can blend any of these techniques (NLP, Mudras, Speech Control) to amplify what we are bringing into being on the physical plane.

If you don't know palmistry or mudras for particular deities that you work with, then work with the following ideas. The first idea is to work with what you know. I have perceived that most people are familiar how to make the word "Okay" using their fingers. If you're not familiar with this, it is bending the pointer finger on a hand to where the tip of it touches the tip of the thumb on the same hand, making it one big circle, or "O." Leave the other three fingers on that hand extended upright, and there have it: your first mudra! An exercise to use is to work this into your day-to-day skill set, and in the beginning, just get in the habit of doing it once a day. After this becomes rote, then increase it to twice a day. When this is mastered, you can then begin to explore the use of other hand gestures that you may know. If you don't know any, then this is an opportune time to discover more about them, and begin to use new ones that are applicable to different situations in your life. As you incorporate them into your daily communication, it would be easiest to use the same system revealed above. From here on out it becomes something for you to research when you choose, as you will.

On a slightly related note, there is something funny to be aware of. I believe we are all familiar with the middle finger gesture that people use, that is widely considered rude in common society. You know, it's the middle finger of either hand extended, while the rest of the digits are folded in on the palms, so it sticks up alone. The funny thing about that is that in palmistry that is the finger associated with Saturn! Hence, when you receive that, you are receiving Saturn from someone. The ultimate joke is on the person casting that towards you, though, because Saturn is the planet that is associated with karma, so when they do that, they are creating karma of a type associated with the action. Thus they are creating their own headaches down the road. Ha!

Another fun mudra to note comes to us from the world of heavy metal music, and is commonly called the "horned hand." Sometimes the thumb is out, and sometimes the thumb is tucked in to the palm. Regardless, though, this mudra bears mentioning here because there is something else attached to this that has been a gift from popular culture. By being called the horned hand, or the hand gesture of the devil, this gesture has become tied into the energy of Baphomet. Baphomet is way too complex being to be addressed here, but suffice to say for our purposes that he is part of the origin of the Christian devil. I have found it very useful in certain situations that I found myself in to invoke this mudra for various reasons: to ground me, to keep me focused on that exact moment, and/or to remember to enjoy my current situation. It brings my mind back to all things related to Baphomet, and thus I use it to increase personal power as applicable to the situations. It is interesting to see how society has given us tools to work with to execute our true Will, isn't it? The horned hand is recognized by most, if not all, but how it will be understood depends upon the situation, and thus this mudra actually illustrates very clearly what I was discussing before about subcultures.

In the heavy metal culture, the horned hand means something extremely different than it does to Christian zealots. In the heavy metal subculture in particular, it is seen as a sign of acknowledgement, which in the Christian zealot subculture it is seen as something to be avoided, or even insulting to experience. This reinforces what I was saying earlier about how a subculture is seen as a culture by those that are involved in it. In the heavy metal subculture, it is simply a "culture." This is true of most forms of music and the adherents to its associated lifestyle.

Like every culture, they have their codes of ethics, preferred methods of behavior, and ways of communication that are generally not understood by people on the outside. Words also take on a double entendre type of meaning as well, so it is wise to watch what you say. This also means that it is wise to watch what you say if you are in the culture itself.

We all now have a clear understanding of the basic science behind vocalization and hearing, so let us proceed with what to do with this knowledge. After all, so far all we've done is discuss the science behind communication, and as we all know, there are two distinct parts to everything: theory and practice. All of the knowledge in the world doesn't mean anything if we can't put it to good use in our day-to-day lives. It is only when we apply what we know to our everyday lives that we practice alchemy and achieve wisdom. Only then do we truly accelerate our spiritual journey. Until then, we are simply becoming comfortable in our own individual skins, and as we get older, the attention focuses more on applying what we know, rather than accumulating any knowledge we come across. It's all about the discipline and the focus. Working with vocal magick is also making a commitment to the self to take control of life, and to live a life greater than we thought possible. The criteria of our success are up to us, and this freedom can empower us in a way that we previously didn't think possible. The information in these chapters also gives all of us a basic consensual platform to work from.

Now, on to part two, and putting an end to using such phrases as "vibrated by the initiator" and so forth. Bah!

# Chapter 4
## Universal and Karmic Laws

Having explored the basics of the underlying theory, we can now start to discuss magickal applications. Most of these applications will be coming from a Western Tradition magical standpoint, but there will also be modern esotericism intermingled throughout the text which comes from a blending of Eastern and Western thought. Now that we have established a solid background and working platform in section 1, we are going to move into a more fluid current, beginning with karma and its symbiotic relationship with language and communication, and the ways these correlate with each other, yet remain independent. If you don't believe in karma, this book is going to be a challenge to understand. I am taking the very definitive stance that karma is real, and while a reader of this book may not believe in karma, it believes in you.

The word "karma" is a Sanskrit term and concept, and roughly translates to "deed" or "action" in English. Thus, on one level it is a way of life rather than some sort of code, but on another, subtler level, it draws our attention to the idea that all causes have effects. While it is an Eastern concept at its root, it is commonly used in various portions of the Western tradition and in modern spirituality. Karma has been studied over the centuries, and because of this, it has been codified and clarified. Karma is not just one simple thing, but rather a system of thinking that it would be wise to integrate into life. It is commonly said, as I did above, that even if you don't believe in karma, it believes in you. Thus if you see karma as a clarification of the cause and effect principle, it is easy to understand how it is always in play, whether we believe in it or not, or even if we are aware of it or not. It is much more than the Golden Rule, which roughly translates into "do unto others as you would have them do unto you." While this is the most common perception, it is only the tip of the iceberg.

There are twelve universal laws of karma that I am going to analyze to illustrate their relevance to why language and communication should be carefully handled. There are many other universal laws that could be used to illustrate what I am trying to convey, but since these are quite common, these are the ones I'll use. On the Tree of Life, Karma corresponds to Geburah[12]. The Lords of Karma reside at Geburah and the Ascended Masters are at Chesed[13], so therefore I will be dealing with each of them in their appropriate context. Everyone knows the most common law: "As you sow, so shall you reap", which is precisely why I will not give it too much more attention than I gave it earlier. After all, the devil is in the details, and there are eleven other details to pick apart and make air tight through the course of this book!

Suffice to say that the above law is also known as the Great Law[14] or the Law of Cause and Effect. When it comes down to almost anything karmic, the basis of it is the above law. If you sow hate, then hate will be attracted to you. If you sow a particular lifestyle, that is what will be drawn to you. Of course there are extrapolations possible and exceptions to this, but in a broad sense the above expression is the core. In essence this law is a fancy way of saying "you get what you give." Thus it becomes clear that it is wise to watch what we project so that we attract the healthiest and right things to us.

---

[12] Geburah or Gevurah is the the fifth sephira, associated with strict adherence to the laws of the cosmos and the capacity to enforce the will.

[13] Chesed is the fourth sephira, considered the first to emerge from the realm of the divine. It is often translated "loving-kindness".

[14] Where do I get these names? A google search pulled up hundreds of pages on the Internet, and most used the wording above. The laws I discuss here are compiled from many of said pages.

The next law to be addressed is the Law of Creation: In order for life to happen we must participate in it. We are one with the universe both inside and outside ourselves. Our outside state of affairs can give us clues as to our inner state, and vice versa, and thus we must always continue being and doing ourselves to achieve greatest understanding. Here is where I'll first mention the Microcosm and Macrocosm. "As Above, So Below". According to Hermetic thought, Hermes Trismegistus gave us that aphorism two millennium ago and truer words couldn't have been spoken. This karmic law also reminds us that life doesn't just happen on its own, but rather it takes our active participation to bring it into being. If we choose to keep our interaction with life to a minimum, then we will have a minimalistic life. If we get over-engaged in life we may find that we run the risk of suffering burnout. Either way, we get out of life what we put into it, so if we don't like our results, it's up to us to change our approach, and the easiest way to change it is through communication. By communicating with others, we put ourselves in a position to create more and better opportunities to maximize our spiritual growth.

This is also where language can be applied. The easiest tool to use at our disposal, being humans, is our voice. Not only is it one of the most versatile tools, it is also one of the most effective. Every sound that comes out of our mouths is heard by something. Whether the receiver is in physical form or not, walks on four legs, flies, swims, or moves by some other means, we are acknowledged every time we use that particular tool. The level of vibrations that the vocal chords work on is tuned to that particular frequency that can affect the most change in our physical surroundings. What a beautiful instrument! It can also be, besides that effectual, a few other adjectives: Subtle, blunt, and hard-to-control.

To some, this may seem a daunting thing at first, but the same factors that make it seem daunting are the reasons that it is empowering. While it may seem like a lot of work, the greater the life lived, the more responsible we can and should become. There is constantly someone hearing what we are saying, even if that being is not physical. If we practice responsible energy cleansing techniques, then we know that the non-physical beings are ones that are there to assist our greatest growth and good. However, if we're not energetically responsible, then those non-physical beings that hear us may seem scary; we may even attract or create those that do not have our best interests in mind. Ultimately, it is up to us to determine what non-physical beings hear us, so we should assume our personal responsibility and claim our personal power.

**I cannot stress enough the importance of speech!** If you are not well versed in controlling your voice, try the technique listed below.

When you awake in the morning and you are doing your morning rituals, say this little affirmation to yourself to get in the habit of being aware of what comes out of your mouth: "I ask for guidance in speech and alertness in attention to my impact on my environment." If this affirmation doesn't work, then don't be afraid to make your own with the same goal in mind. Make sure to do this every day. I realize that it may be hard at first to get yourself in the habit, but when you do, you may find that you not only gain greater control over your speech, but that you also may cultivate internal discipline on a greater level, which can then be applied to many different situations.

By stating this, you are declaring to whatever paradigm you subscribe to, deities if applicable, that you have a basic understanding of this world of maya. The term "maya" here is not referring to a native group of people, but rather is a term from Hinduism. In Hinduism, maya is a word that means "illusion." Reality is an illusion, after all, and because of this it can be affected in a very plastic and holographic manner, if you choose. In essence, all of life and existence is fractal in nature. Each time you convey a message from a belief stance, you are also declaring that you are assuming a responsibility for what you do and say. For example, if you say you believe that something in your life is occurring for the better, you may find that you are immediately challenged on whether or not that is actually true. You are also beginning to proceed on the path to co-creation with the unmanifest[15], as you choose what you do and do not speak into being. After you use this for a time you will see other effects. The latter effects you will see are more tangible and manifest.

## More Karmic Tools

As you work with these techniques, the clues I mentioned in the above law will make themselves more pronounced and easier to spot and interpret. If every other word that comes out of your mouth is something negative, either towards yourself or others, then don't be surprised if those that are attracted to you constantly surround you with that energy. This is a common root cause of people being in negative situations. Often times what we need to work with is our immediate environment and this can be the most profound situation to modify. In some cases there is only so much that can be done, but what can be done is still very profound and powerful. By being aware of our situations as we move through life, we put ourselves in a greater position of personal empowerment. By paying attention to every situation all the time, we strengthen our minds to handle those situations that we encounter. In other words, it is wise to guard against becoming

---

[15] Here again, as in previous chapters, this is a generic term until we clarify and define it later.

subconscious in our routines. If we don't think about what we are doing on a moment-by-moment basis, we fall into repetitive patterns that may not be good for our greatest growth and health. Also, this behavior is potentially dangerous, as we are more likely to fall prey to physical accidents when we assume that we know all about where we are in our comfortable environment and stop paying attention. How many times have you stubbed your toe when you rounded a corner too quickly in your home environment, or something similar? By being consciously aware of as much of each situation as possible, we keep the mind alert. As has been said many times in psychic cycles: "Awareness is the beginning of cultivating your psychic skills." The more we are aware, the more we open ourselves up to the natural evolution of our inherent psychic abilities, which vary from person to person.

This leads us into the Law of Attraction. It is not technically a law of karma, but rather a Universal Law. I will be only briefly giving any attention to the Universal Laws, as they are far more vast and complicated. In all honesty, they deserve their own book (or several books!). This one, however, bears mention because of its immediate relevance and the support it gives the karmic laws. The essence of the Law of Attraction is thus: Like attracts like. If you are a magician, you will find yourself more and more surrounded by magickal types of people. If you are negative, you will find yourself surrounded by negativity, and negativity drawn to you. Etc., etc. The vibrations coming out of the mouth, which are rooted in the vibrations of the mind, define the things that will share your space with you. The law of attraction has become popular over the last few years, but the secret component behind it lies in the actions that you're willing to take to manifest the results of your attraction. In other words, if you're not prepared to make the necessary adjustments or pay the necessary prices, then you're not going to manifest what it is that you want easily, if at all.

Next on the list is The Law of Growth. In essence, it is this: In order for us to grow, we must affect the only true constant in our lives: ourselves. The people, places, and other things in our lives will grow with us. Granted, as we grow, the transition out of some of those relationships and interactions may be painful. That effect is due to other issues, which I will only mention here in passing: the pain of losing things we are emotionally attached to. This has to do with the emotional body, but it bears mentioning. This law has also been paraphrased as "Wherever you go, there you are." As we travel and grow, we never lose our path per se, but rather it is constantly with us, no matter where we find ourselves. Often, people think that they have fallen off of their path, but actually their path has simply changed into a form that they did not find or in keeping with what they expected. The path hasn't left them, but they simply temporarily lost the ability to spot the path.

The easiest way to begin the road to taking a more active role in our lives is to know our limitations and strengths. We must keep in mind is that we truly do only have ultimate control over ourselves, and nothing more. We can co-create and change our environment, but if the Unmanifest says things are going to go a certain direction, then they are. Of course we have free will, being humans, but that will must be used responsibly and towards higher vibrational ends. We can dictate how we proceed, but the direction we proceed can either be viewed as a decree from the Unmanifest to be followed blindly, or a possibility to co-create that path with the Unmanifest. If we view the decree from the Unmanifest from the stance of a helpless victim, we open the door for a whole different realm of existence: a door which most would find undesirable.

Speaking of undesirable doors, our next law touches on that: the Law of Humility. What you refuse to accept will persist for you. I have had many discussions with a dear friend of mine about this. I like to view this law as a law of initiation. Meditation on this law will reveal many levels that it affects, and thus the many possible discussions. This law is rather subtle and thought provoking. In essence, as we refuse to deal with things that need dealt with from a growth or karmic angle, those things stalk us and force us to confront them. Each time they are not dealt with lends them more power and energy, and the "trials become more severe"[16]. As one grows on their path, bigger and more intricate ordeals and tests come. These have their roots in either the karmic or the initiator reasons listed above. It must always be remembered that when these growth opportunities arrive, we must embrace the challenge they present. We can, as governed by free will, see such instances as problems, but if we do we immediately give them energy. I don't know about you, but I don't like to give energy on a subconscious level to anything. I would rather give conscious energy to what I choose. These growth opportunities are simply tests by the Unmanifest to see how we've grown. Keeping in mind that we are never given more than we can handle, these opportunities should not be viewed as things that are meant to propel us backwards, but rather chances for us to shine. By being aware of our language, we become more aware of our interaction with the Unmanifest, and thus more aware of the subtle currents in our individual paths.

Being aware of those currents on our path, both subtle and not, brings us to two laws: The Law of Connection and the Law of Focus. The Law of Connection is simply that you must make sure every little detail gets done, no matter how inconsequential it may seem, or where its falls within the creation process. Everything is inter-related, although we may not see the relationship.

---

[16] This is a paraphrase from The Book of The Law, chapter 1, verse 38.

The Law of Focus states that when our attention is not focused on spiritual matters, we succumb to thoughts of lower vibrations: greed, hate, envy, and so on.

## Tools of the Non-Physical Kind

Our voice is the most versatile tool (besides our minds) to effect change on a very tangible level. While the vibration of the tangible and manifested world that we live in is, conceptually speaking, a lower vibration, it is not something that we should deal with from a lower vibrational standpoint. To bring about the most positive and transformative change, we need to come at things from the plane above the one we choose to affect[17]. Therefore, while the manifested world is on a lower vibration than other worlds, we shouldn't lower ourselves to that level to work with it. If we follow the Law of Focus, it empowers us on our journey.

Man is a tool-using creature, and by using our natural tools wisely, we can get further along our soul's path more quickly than if we didn't. Simply, these two laws address awareness as a tool itself, and through greater awareness we can raise our consciousness more effectively than if we just put our head down and charged through situations in life. While sometimes it is necessary to simply bull through and get to the other side, doing so with a conscious awareness will make that even more effective.

Related to this and to the Law of Humility is the next karmic law: The Law of Change. History will always repeat itself until we learn the lessons we need to learn from it. The true trick to this law is being able to spot the repetition. If we cannot identify the situation, then we cannot correct that in ourselves which contributes to it; thus we return, as always, to awareness. By increasing our

---

[17] Dion Fortune, in her book "Circuit of Force", goes into great detail about this.

awareness, we are sharpening our skills to perceive. By sharpening those skills, we are sharpening our communication skills as both sender and receiver.

As change comes about through our awareness and actions, so, too, does the next karmic law to be discussed: The Law of Giving and Hospitality. Essentially, it states that if we believe something to be true, at some point we will have to demonstrate that truth. This is putting what we say we've learned into practice. This is another law that I have had extensive conversations about. It also ties into the discussion in chapter X of this book: the example of the sky being blue. If you believe the sky is blue, then there will come a time when you will have to stand up for that belief. If you believe that there is only one path to enlightenment, you will meet people and situations that challenge that belief. This is not a negative situation. Rather, in puts the emphasis on us to be secure in our beliefs, and be clear on them as well.

There are two laws that tie into each other so closely that they bear mentioning together: they are the Law of Patience and Reward, and the Law of Significance and Inspiration. Symbiotically, they are thus: You get out of something the amount of work you put into it, and what is worth having is not necessarily easy to obtain. Both of these laws address hard work, initial toil, and the price to pay for such accomplishments. I address them both here, together, to illustrate this point about speech: If all things worth having are worth the work, and the rewards will come in their own time, then why make the road any harder than it already is? We make the road harder by being mindless in our speech, and letting things flop out of our mouths that build up energy and work against us. If we watch what we say, and are very careful about what we are working towards, then a road that might have been impossible has now become simply difficult. Never forget that the Unmanifest wants to see us happy.

Two laws remain to consider. The Law of Here and Now indicates that whenever we look back and live in the past, we are prevented, through our own will's choice, from having new situations and experiences. We remain fixed on what was. The Law of Responsibility states that whenever there is something wrong, there is something wrong within us. Since we are part of the whole of this reality, what is happening in us affects what is happening around us, and vice versa. As above, so below; as within, so without.

Fundamentally, they are two very tough laws to accept, but are worth it when they are understood. The first, Law of the Here and Now, does not mean not to look back at all, as one might guess. It means that we should analyze and learn our lessons from past situations, but we should not judge our future on them, nor cling to those memories as a definition of our subjective realities. This law is almost the opposite of the psychological principle of classical conditioning. If we touch a stove when we are young, got burnt, touched the stove again and got burnt again, then we began to learn through repeated action and the pain associated with it that touching the stove in that way is bad. This karmic law doesn't contradict that, but it does require meditation. If said stove burned us when we were younger, and we learned not to touch the stove in that fashion, and that was the end of it, we are missing half of the picture. Now that we are older than when that instance happened, we realize that it those events came about through carelessness or ignorance on our part. Does that mean that, to this day, we shouldn't touch a stove in that fashion? No. Now that we are more experienced, we understand the principles behind said youthful stove burn, and can adapt to them.

That is the true point of this law. If we got burned when we were younger, we shouldn't accept that, stopping analysis at that level. We need to go a step further to truly grasp what is at work here. Yes, look back into the past to understand it, but don't live in the past, for that prevents utilizing the energies of the present and creating the future.

The Law of Responsibility is clear enough, but I will explore it briefly. It is one of the toughest laws to work with because it puts ultimate blame on us, where I believe it should be. No finger pointing. No excuses. It's a very straightforward law, but very powerful when understood and used properly. When we accept that mantle, we are rearranging our mind to reach a different level on a higher vibrational plane, and this can lead into a greater awareness, which will help with speech and our creation of reality on an individual level.

I realize that this chapter covered a lot of ground very briefly, and did not go into great depth, but I chose to keep it brief to stay true to my focus upon the power of language. Understanding that there are these karmic laws at work now gives us a framework for the rest of our study. It should be an aim to work within these laws, accepting their guidance, and not be at cross-purposes with them and spend all our energies struggling against the inevitable. Of course this is a free will zone, so one can ignore them if one so desires, but their effects will be prevalent enough over time through observation and awareness. The quickest way to understand these laws is through the tool of the voice; to get a working understanding of the laws, it would be best to begin with communication and study its effects. Since we have established that there is always an audience, there is always the opportunity to learn from these karmic laws in action.

### Double Entendre Fun!

Double entendres can be quite fun and useful to use when you're speaking to someone, but beware because they can also get you in a lot of trouble, and can send mixed signals to the universe, making manifestation harder. Double entendres are words that have two distinct different meanings and applications. For example, the word "sage" can be used as a double entendre. It can either mean a wise person, or it can refer to the sage plant that is commonly used in smudging.

It quickly becomes obvious that there are many benefits to using these types of words. To begin with, innocently, they can be playful fun when shared with your audience. However, they can also provide barriers to clear conversation if they are used in a sloppy fashion. They have been used through the years to convey hidden and subtle messages to people to influence how the audience sees the transmitter. A common manifestation of this has been in occult literature, and has to do with literary blinds that some authors use to veil messages that are only available for those that can figure them out, or to those that are shown them. Yes, double entendres and literary blinds occur in many different areas of literature, and if you take the time, you can find quite profound messages hidden between the lines. This same approach can be applied to vocal magick, in that by increasing your vocabulary, you put yourself in a position to utilize this very potent tool.

The first thing to do if you want to begin working with double entendres is to increase your knowledge of words themselves. This can include everything from simply freshening up your knowledge of definitions for the words that you already use, to expanding in new directions using a thesaurus or other tool, to studying another language entirely. Sometimes the words have been in front of us all along, but we only knew one definition of them. Other times, this research leads us into the discovery of subtle and subconscious patterns we may have when it comes to speech. I have found that using an accurate word beats using a word that requires many adjectives. If you decide to expand your vocabulary using new words, then it would be wise to incorporate one or two new words a day in applicable situations. I say "applicable situations" because sometimes people will use a new word that they found just to impress people, and it becomes obvious to the audience that this word is not fluidly incorporated into the speaker's vibration. Hence it looks like that person going out of their way to impress them, and usually people are turned off by that behavior.

At the best, though, double entendres can be quite valuable. On one hand, their use challenges the audience to know their own vocabulary. On the other, though, you can use this technique to see who truly understands what you're saying, and the message that you're sharing. For example, if you use a word that has two meanings, and 90% of the people that hear it miss the meaning that you intend, then you can either use a different word, or choose to focus your attention on the 10% that do understand what you're saying.

Double entendres can also be very good for defusing situations that we may find ourselves wanting to resolve. Sexual inuendos usually have a lot of double entendre play with them, and in the proper company and context, this can be quite comedic. However, it is also worth being careful with this because sometimes the audience receives a message that you didn't intend. For example, while you may be playful about it, others may take it seriously, and this creates a situation that can have serious karmic repercussions. If this should happen, the responsibility falls on our shoulders (not theirs) because we went into the situation knowing what we were doing. If we don't take into account the psychological orientation of the person or people that heard us use those words, we risk creating difficulties, miscommunications, and damaging our relationships with those people. I have frequently used awareness of these facts to separate those that are serious about their personal development versus those that just treat it as a hobby to be practiced, but not lived.

Above I mentioned that using double entendres can be karmically sketchy, at best. Let me take a moment to explain this. I have a very simple philosophy towards life and the concept of morality overall. Universal and karmic laws are called that because they are absolutes in their execution of results. Anything beyond that is human projection upon any given situation based on the individual ego. Hence, if you are mindful of universal and karmic laws, then you are living in line with the world that we all inhabit. Of course this does not mean that I don't follow other laws, but rather spiritually, psychologically, these are the ones of utmost importance to me. If you use words that are double entendres, you may end up tying yourself up in vagueness, and according to these principles, that comes with a steep price. While generally this works out okay, the challenge comes in when we watch for manifestation from our work. Sometimes, if things are too grey, nothing manifests, which can be a source of frustration. Thus what we are left with is a sense of knowing when we want to walk the grey area between the laws, and when it is better to simply be direct. The funny thing about that, though, is that we're all brought full circle back to one of the early lessons on the spiritual path, which is the lesson of discernment. It's interesting how the ideology of the master is the same as that of the student, isn't it: "Chop wood, carry water."

# Chapter 5
# Semantics!

Now that we have explored the laws of karma as a working frame for the mechanisms of vocal magick, let us at last turn our attention to a more concrete topic: semantics. How is all of this used and abused in everyday life? Why should one care about what comes out of the mouth? What is its weight, anyway? After all, as is commonly thought, *"they're just words"*.

If you believe that they are just words, put this book down. Go back and seriously think about events that have happened to you, things people have said, praise and criticism and even abuse you have received, and see if you can actually believe that those things were just words. Find the root of your avoidance and heal that wound. Only when that wound is healed will it be worthwhile for you to pick this book up from this spot and continue. "Sticks and stones may break my bones, but words will never hurt me" is one of those lies told to children for others' convenience; it is a fundamental denial of the power of the connection that vibrates between beings.

The most powerful tool you have at your disposal is your language, and it is always in your possession. Every thought you think, every word you say is heard by an entity. After all, as is commonly taught, "thoughts are things." It is not my intent to make you paranoid, but rather to impress upon you the need for personal responsibility. How many times have you said something and then within days (or less!) been confronted with a seemingly coincidental response from the universe to said subject? Here's a more or less common example of what I mean:

> #1: "Did you hear about what happened to Sam?"
> #2: "No, what happened?"
> #1: "She lost her mid-term project when her computer crashed."
> #2: "Oh yeah?"
> #1: "Yeah. If I'd been her, I would've backed it up and printed it out, too!"

Can the next step be guessed? You got it. Within a short time span after this conversation, #1 has a crash happen (or similar event that could've been avoided, but was equally disastrous), and is in the same predicament as Sam. The extenuating circumstances may be different, but the root (and the stress from the event) is the same. By affirming in conversation that they would certainly follow a particular course, #1 made a very loud statement to the universe: "Put me in a similar position so I can handle it in the way that I believe would be the *right* way." This is of course the sort of claim that indicates that someone might need to work on their relationship with their ego, but it also comes down to a question of their intent.

Of course I'm sure such a disaster was not #1's intent, but while the universe may be fueled by intent, a karmic law was invoked here, specifically the law of giving and of hospitality. If we believe something to be true, then at some point we will have to step up and walk the walk, instead of just talking the talk. Since the karmic law was so blatantly called upon, that triggered the situation to arise to force #1 to walk the walk.

If #1 had just been a little more careful with the wording, they might have avoided being placed in a similar position. Avoiding positions that may not be in your best interests through proper language control is truly the heart of this book. If, by awareness and cautious control over our language, we can put ourselves in better situations as people, then why not be more aware? I can't speak for the average reader, but I for one have enough karma to work through in this life without adding more to it by not paying attention to what I say! None for me, thanks, I'm driving!

## Clichés

Now that you've got the picture, we'll proceed to the nuts and bolts. The best way I've found to gain control over language is to master my native tongue, and secondly to learn foreign languages. Once you master your native tongue, you have a better grasp of words and sentence structure, and through this knowledge you can place your words more appropriately and poignantly. By arranging them in that fashion you will quickly notice a particular pattern. You will likely find that you start sounding like an automaton because you repeat commonly used words too often, and you feel like you blend into the background of peoples' minds, not standing out in any way, shape, or form. When you have reached that realization the fun begins!

After you master your native tongue, you are in a position to branch out and learn other languages. You may even find that learning another language illuminates things that you found confusing in your native tongue! One of the more interesting points about learning multiple languages is that you start to understand the glue that binds all language together: the conveyance of concepts, utmost and foremost. Thus, once you learn a second language it becomes easier to learn a third, and so on and so forth. All languages have basic concepts that are universal in nature, and a lot of the time this reflects common situations that we as humans find ourselves in. For example, let's look at the idea and concept of the bathroom. Here in the United States it is known as a bathroom commonly, but in other parts of the world it has different terms. A slang term in the UK is "loo." In the United States Navy, the term is "the head." In a lot of places in Eastern Europe it is known as a "Water Closet," sometimes expressed as "the WC". However, regardless of the language or culture that we find ourselves in, all humans need somewhere to excrete, and thus with little to no knowledge of a particular language we can navigate at least the basics of society very easily. If we understand that the concept of the bathroom is universal, then we realize that all societies will have a term that identifies that space. Hence it becomes easy to start to navigate the culture, and thus a key to learning a language is revealed. By studying concepts that are universal, we get to the underpinnings of communication, and in some ways we begin to return to that one prototypal root language that was mentioned earlier. Obviously this isn't enough to successfully learn a language, but this is one of the better secret keys that are out there to understand *how* to learn multiple languages, and thus multiple cultures.

A side effect of this is that by being aware of your vocabulary control and skills, you pave the way to do better medium work in the future, since a channeled entity is limited by the vocabulary of the medium (as well as other minor mitigating factors). If the medium doesn't have a particular word in their vocabulary, then they don't necessarily have control over said concept, or a thorough enough understanding to convey that concept from the channeled entity to others. The idea of words, especially names, granting control over items is an age-old magical principle that has been addressed extensively in many schools of thought, from ceremonial magic to fairy tales. One could try to argue that this is not the case, since the subconscious works on symbols. However, anyone who has done medium work in the past can testify that when doing such work, you would rather be coming from a conscious stance than a subconscious one. Why is that?

From a conscious stance you have more capacity for control, even if you are a fly on the wall during the channeling. If it were all subconscious, then that could be very good, as in the case of Edgar Cayce, or it could be very bad, with the entity's messages being perverted by lack of skill or, worse, the influence of a hostile entity getting free access to the physical world. Granted, Cayce's work wasn't necessarily all developed from a subconscious stance, but a large portion of it was.

Austin Osman Spare is in the same boat as Cayce, pursuing a path to magical power through the unconscious, and look at the results he produced with his automatic drawings! We have a spectrum to work within when it comes to understanding the interplay between language and symbols. While these two men performed on this spectrum in a way that was more subconscious than conscious, they still arrived at the destination of symbol usage in a very powerful way; Cayce could draw answers to questions from his well-trained intuition, and the artistic work of Spare is foundational to the development of modern sigil magic. In this book I put the focus on conscious control of language, but these two individuals reveal the other end of the spectrum, and isn't it interesting how both ends achieve the same goal through opposite methods?

## Reality Creation

Bringing into being the principle, belief, and paradigm enhancer that "you create your reality" is the next step. As soon as you reach a conscious awareness of every syllable that comes out of your mouth you realize that by saying anything, you are giving the receiver (or receivers) a way to define and understand you. You are giving them a little piece of your reality with each sentence, guiding their thoughts in a certain direction when they think about you, what you've said, and when they talk to you.

I'm not implying that this dialogue is a beginning (in however as miniscule sense as it seems) of ambition by any means. What I'm saying is this: If one is going to interact with people, one should make sure to paint oneself, through actions and words, in the best and most effective light possible. Keeping in mind that the speaker will be expected to act according to their words by the laws of karma, espousing purer goals and principles will thus raise one's vibrations. The highest vibration out there right below the godhead is love. This increases one's integrity. Saying what you mean and then walking the talk that comes out of your mouth is of utmost importance in this day and age! Doing what you say is a key to the evolution of mankind, and of the planet! More and more people are becoming cognizant of this and putting it to work for them, so why not tap into the growing current of energy that they are building?

This is where the mastery of the words in the language you are using comes in. Say, for example, that whenever you converse with someone, you want them to walk away from the conversation thinking "That is a very conscientious person", then the words you must choose are words that feed that particular thoughtform. I enjoy perusing a thesaurus occasionally to find new ways to express myself. Self-expression can be a very beautiful thing when applied purposefully. It can also be said self-expression can be a very terrible thing when used inappropriately. This is where intent comes into play heavily, which we will address in a minute. Suffice to say that if you want people to look at you in a particular light then you need to work with that idea and portray yourself appropriately, choosing your words and expressions of meaning so that they match that appearance.

Isn't it funny how so many concepts that we are introduced to as children really hold deeper motivations and meanings? I can remember teachers and parents telling me to watch what I say when I was growing up as a young boy. Of course I didn't listen to them because I was a youngster and didn't know what I know now, but it happened nonetheless. In my humble opinion, it is a very beautiful thing to see all the intricacies of life weave together to form this beautiful reality we create every day. The tapestry of existence is something to marvel at, if you ever stop and look at it.

This technique can also cover more psychological and therapeutic concepts such as self-love and self-talk. If, when you are frustrated, you talk down to yourself, then that particular thought form takes on energy, and begins to become the norm as opposed to the exception. That's fine if you want that in your paradigm, but it's a little too lower vibrational to me. Perhaps you might now understand where I was coming from earlier when I said to shelve this book if you hadn't dealt with that particular issue. When one begins to take full responsibility for their language and usage (and, by default, their life), one opens the door with each sentence to a very powerful healing medicine. This healing medicine is put into practice through language, and can bring about very powerful changes. Granted it can also open the door for a rough road if one is not accustomed to self-criticism, and doesn't have the strength to persevere through the changes. On that tangent, you could say that language is also a very powerful sword. So, what's the difference between a pen and a sword again?

Of course one could take the contrary route, using words to wound rather than to heal. Conflict is something that is often caused by language and words, and is wise to remember that not all people that work with language in this fashion are coming at things from a space of love and healing. Some people use language to cause conflict and damage, and if we are aware of these people, we put ourselves in a better position to deal with them when we encounter them. We can also see their weaknesses, as the words people use reveal parts about their mental programming and base psychological perspective. We may discover that someone that seems like a good person on the surface is actually a not so nice person when it comes to loving themselves. By working with both of these concepts, we can also begin to develop the skill of telepathy, which is best discovered by anticipation. When we can anticipate where the conversation is going next, we can put our thought processes a step ahead of the receiver/s. All it takes to enact this is mental clarity and self-control. A strong dose of patience is also preferred!

We can proceed no further without addressing the question of intention and its function within our use of language. Let's say that after working with this subject you realize that inflection plays a huge role in the nature of communication. This is a psychologically proven fact. I am reminded of an episode of the cable TV show named "Penn & Teller: Bullshit". An episode of theirs dealt with language extensively. The focus of that episode was upon curse words, and the acceptability of some words in a public setting. I suggest you track down that episode if you're interested in more information about this specific topic. I want to just mention that a very applicable part of that was when they discussed how you say things as opposed to what you say. If you say "I hate you" in a very loving, sweet, grandmotherly manner, then what energy is that sending? The true answer to that question is a very well guarded esoteric secret, and is a Rosetta Stone to many other wonders of the magickal universe, but it is well worth your time to contemplate it now and consider the nature of the vibrations that such a juxtaposition creates.

Suffice to say that what you say is as important as how you say it. If you say positive words, but you use an inflection that is negative, then how can you expect to get anywhere with your audience? The message bearer is then sending mixed signals, and that does not help support the message bearer's paradigm, or the receiver's paradigm. It also borders on hypocrisy, which is already in abundance on this planet, and is antithetical to walking your talk.

Up to this point in this chapter I've tried to illustrate different reasons and situations to express why one would want to be mindful of their speech. Now I'm going to change gears for a short time. I'm going to address the concept of non-verbal communication for those of you out there that subscribes to the eastern concept of "be-ing". How is a book on language going to benefit those who keep language to a minimum, or who are coming from a Buddhistic stance? Honestly, it's not. Not in the conventional sense of benefiting at least. However, this work does cover what exactly is going on out there with regards to western spirituality and its growth over the last forty years or so. Perhaps strategy is conveyed when it comes to picking and choosing your use of silence and words?

For example the state of be-ing is very different than the state of doing, and language is very commonly oriented around doing rather than being. Meditation is an excellent illustration of my point. When one meditates, there is generally no language involved. You can meditate (or lead meditations) while talking, but those are more the exceptions to the rule rather than the rule itself. Even when one is not seeking a no-mind meditation, often the goal is to allow verbal thoughts to surface and pass through the mind without becoming a process of internal chatter. In the state of be-ing, one goes deeply inward on a very fine body level. This is a wonderful way to master communication, since all communication begins on an internal level. This is also an excellent way to enhance already present communication skills, since by reflection one can gain wisdom on the experiences of every day life. This reflection leads to more awareness of one's self, and the state of affairs surrounding one's life. Through such observations one can become more in control of their reality.

In this light, one who walks the eastern path can benefit from seeing that there is a consciousness raising going on that is not only beneficial, but also necessary to preserve heritage and culture. As the world homogenizes, certain things are at risk of being lost. One of those things is ancient techniques and esoteric secrets. The west is at the front of global culture. Don't believe me? Just watch the news from around the world and see what social moves other countries are making right now that emulate western world trends and fashions.

To wrap this chapter up, I would like to share with you, the reader, a technique that is highly effective, but not for the weak of heart or thin of skin. This technique is a derivative of a technique taught by the World Teacher Aleister Crowley, and addressed in several of his books, including *Magick in Theory and Practice*, *Magick Without Tears*, and other non-Crowley (but influenced by him) titles, such as John Symonds *The Great Beast* (complete with pictures!) and *The Magical Dilemma of Victor Neuberg* by Jean Overton Fuller.

The technique that Crowley taught involved a razor blade; however I prefer a rubber band. I received the rubber band idea received from a very dear friend of mine (you know who you are!). Here's the technique:

Set yourself a goal. For example, when I used the technique, I was in the process of removing the ego from conversation.

Secondly, put the rubber band on your wrist. If you feel motivated, write on the rubber band what it is you are working with.

Third, every time the concept comes up that you are working with, snap the rubber band against your wrist to associate pain with the idea.

Here's the way it worked for me. Every time I felt the impulse to say the word "I," I would snap the rubber band against my wrist. The more I phrased sentences with that letter, the harder I snapped the rubber band. Pretty soon, every time I contemplated using the letter "I" as a pronoun to describe myself, every time I focused my language so intensely on myself rather than my principles or what I wished to communicated, I associated this concept with pain. After that I found myself having the impulse to use the letter "I" as a pronoun less and less frequently, except when it was actually critical to what I wanted to communicate.

Then I wrote on the rubber band other ideas, such as negativity and self-doubt, and every time those ideas would enter into my head I would snap the rubber band in the same manner as before. Lo and behold, over time, those ideas left my paradigm as well! This is a remarkably effective technique, but if one has a low pain tolerance, then a different tool might be used to produce the same effect. As I stated earlier, when Crowley did this, he promoted a razor blade slash across the wrist, and in Symond's book *The Great Beast*, there are pictures of the cuts on the arms of Victor Neuberg who did it that way. A gentler technique was recommended by Israel Regardie, who suggested using a stage illusionist's palm buzzer. All you have to do is keep it in your pocket, and every time the trigger occurs, you reach in and sting yourself. It delivers a minor electrical shock, but doesn't leave red welts like the rubber band technique could. After all, it may be difficult to explain to loved ones while you have red welts on your wrist and forearms if you use the rubber band method!

Simply take the technique you choose and apply it to language and vocabulary. If you want to rid your vocabulary of the thought form of self-doubt, then every time a thought of self-doubt comes up, snap the rubber band or apply whatever other method you choose. It is amazing in my opinion how quickly this technique can produce positive change. I also strongly suggest writing on the rubber band what it is you are working with, providing a language-based focus for the work, and journaling your progress. After all, if there is no journal, how can one chart their progress on their path? When I used this technique, I saw almost immediate results as long as I had the willpower to follow through on it consistently.

To sum this chapter so far up: Semantics! Semantics! Semantics! The devil (if you believe in one) and/or God (if you believe in one) and Goddess (if you believe in one) is in the details, and we live in a world and at a time when the details are so very important! Out with sloppiness and laziness! In with details and awareness! Viva Revolutione!

## Neutrality

A final piece to the puzzle to consider is of speaking neutrally. This can be a touchy and controversial subject, so be forewarned. Speaking neutrally can be quite the challenge, but the secret to successfully doing this is to remove the ego from conversation. Let's start by discussing adjectives.

Adjectives are words that are used to describe something. For example, in the phrase, "The big experiment," the word "big" is an adjective to describe the experiment itself. While yes, adjectives can be very good to use to describe whatever it is that you're witnessing or conveying, there is a challenge that goes with them. The challenge lies in the fact that they may address something to you, but that may not be applicable in the mind of the person you're conveying the thought to. In other words, what is big to you may be small to someone else. This adds a layer of complexity to your communication, and whenever you add complexity, you add the potential for confusion and misinterpretation. I realize that this can be seen as a minor detail, but it's important for a few different reasons.

The first reason this is important to address is because the more adjectives used, the more your own perspective is revealed. Granted, most times that is the desired effect, but it gives other people the ability to see into how your mind works, and we live in a world where people may use that against you rather than with you. Hence, parsimony in the use of adjectives is a sort of verbal defense mechanism. If you carefully watch your adjectives, you protect yourself from the influence of others. While sometimes it is a good thing to be open to others and what they have to say, this is something that should be approached with caution because the more someone knows about you, the more you've let them into your mind. I also realize that at the extreme, this may sound like paranoia, but that, too, can be guarded against, by using appropriate adjectives, and avoiding others. For example, in the following statement "the blue chair," the word "blue" as an adjective is definitely appropriate as it conveys the color of the chair. However, if you said "the crappy blue chair," then what is revealed to the audience is that you have a negative view on the chair, and possibly on other things in life at well. After all, language defines reality in a lot of ways. Personally, I prefer that others not know how I view things due to the fact that A) I'm a constant work in progress, and my disposition may change daily, if not hourly, and B) I like to keep a tight control on how others perceive my perspective. However, that is just me, so take it with a grain of salt.

The other facet to this is that by being mindful of our adjectives, we can control our own psychological views on things. For example, if we notice we use a lot of negative adjectives, then it is easy for us to ascertain that we are seeing things too negatively, and thus we have a beginning point to grow from. If we can distinguish one chair from another by referring to the one we want as "blue", adding the value judgment of "crappy" is superfluous and unnecessarily introduces lower energies. We discover that we're more negative than we might have thought, and thus have a basic understanding of why things are in our life the way they are. This puts us in greater control of our reality.

Further, when we gain control over our speech, we can begin to increase the magick that is in our life. For example, we can begin using adjectives as a force to draw more mystical and magical experiences to us. I have found this quite effective, as it demonstrates to other people, and to the universe, that we are open to interacting with magick, and we welcome it into our lives. An interesting side note is that in the astrological system, personal communication corresponds to the planet Mercury, and in the western tradition, Mercury is a key component in the process of alchemy, which is the process of turning the lead of the personality self into the gold of the spiritual self. Further, Mercury is in some ways of thinking another form of the magician, Hermes Trismegistus!

Speaking neutrally also puts us in a position to be more dynamic with our speech. For example, if we generally don't use adjectives, then when we use them becomes more pronounced, and will be of greater impact to those that hear the words we speak. In a lot of ways this is verbal strategy, as it becomes easier to make a point, and those points can be made with subtlety and finesse. We no longer have to shout or get extreme when we speak, but rather with just the insertion of one word, we can convey our point to those that are our audience. I have found that a strategically placed adjective can convey more than a raised voice emphasizing a point. This also has a tendency to drive other people to frustration because you're meeting them with intelligence, and they're generally not expecting it, so it puts them back on their heels. When this occurs, you have the psychological high ground, which works the same as in swordplay, in that the person that has the high ground has the advantage.

This does bring us to an important point, though, which is the point of emotional control. Often when people speak about something, they are speaking from a very passionate perspective. While it is wise and good to have an emotional investment in something that you're speaking about, and in life in general, it is just as wise to remain in control of these emotions, for loss of control can lead to all kinds of undesired side effects. Yes, it is wise to honor the emotions, and to not suppress them, but we will also encounter those people and beings that feed off of emotions, and we do not wish to become prey to them. I have discovered that the secret to managing emotions is to recognize that they are there, then to recognize why they are there, and then to cut the energy that is going into them. I realize this sounds easier to say than it really is to implement, and that is true. Often times it is trial and error until we find the methods and techniques that work for us. In this case it is wise to experiment with close friends whom we feel safe around. Then, as we build up emotional self-control, we can go live with other people in our lives, such as bosses at work and the average person in the street that makes us angry.

What happens after the interaction is just as important as what happens in preparation, though. After we are away from the situation that has triggered our emotions, it would be wise to do something with that energy to burn it out of our system. This can be accomplished in many different ways. For example, some people physically work out the energy. Other people punch walls. Obviously there are healthy and unhealthy ways to vent this energy and it is up to each person to discover what works for them. There are plenty of resources out there addressing how to productively use these energy surpluses, both magically focused and not. For now it is simply enough to recognize that after we have exercised control over our emotions and language, we should do something with that energy, not only to honor ourselves, but also to vent the energy so it doesn't unintentionally manifest in our life to our detriment. The most interesting thing about emotions is that if you remove the energy attached to them, they become easier to manage. To some this may appear cold, but in reality it is simply a mature approach to navigating the self and life.

I have found that speaking in a matter of fact way is usually the most applicable approach to take until the situation can be psychologically assessed. This can be dangerous, though, because some people perceive that as condescending or authoritarian, depending on how you roll your views out. This idea comes with a caveat, though, and that is that if you walk the line between confidence and arrogance very well, it becomes a moot point how people perceive that. After all, if this is performed well, you'll speak from a space of confidence, and if others misconstrue that as condescension, then, well, that's karmically on them. Sometimes this is a sliding scale, though, as what is confident to one person is condescending to another, so it is wise to choose and use this technique carefully.

# Chapter 6
## Awareness and Recognition

In the previous chapter we discussed a very direct application of language and very direct consequences. Therefore in this chapter it only stands to reason that we are going to take things a little easier, doesn't it? We could easily maintain directness throughout the whole of this text, but that might not convey the subtlety that can be very useful when it comes to using our language as a form of magick. If you don't believe me, I suggest you study politics, for successful politicians are true wordsmiths in almost every way.

There is a certain level of awareness that has been discussed in passing up to this point of the text, and now would be a great time to address it directly and more in depth. The more aware one is of the language they use, the more one can become an active part of their karmic story. The victim mentality sheds like a second skin. Once an awareness that is backed up by detailed journalizing has been achieved, it becomes second nature to control it after an extended period of time; when it is controlled, the doorway opens to new possibilities, or perhaps it's that one becomes aware of the door that was always there. All that is needed is an awareness of the language that comes out of our mouths every day. Once we master that observation skill, we begin to understand what it means to control our reality. After all, language defines reality[18].

So, as a synopsis, let me put it this way: If you are aware of the language that comes out of your mouth, and are in control of it, then you have an easier time controlling

---

[18] This has been a common debate among scholars for years. Does language define reality? I'm choosing to say yes.

and building your reality. The only thing that has to be done is to control the mind and the tongue. Language is a wonderful tool for achieving reality creation. All that is left to learn are the laws of karma and universal laws. While I have already covered the karmic laws, universal laws still remain to be discussed. Am I going to teach you those here and now? Um, no. Why not? If I gave every key away, then I would have to answer for that karmically. Why not just encourage you to seek the answers yourselves? In brief, though, universal laws are laws that govern the cosmos that apply to all; hence the term "universal." As we as a species develop, more and more laws are discovered, and more and more applications can be found for them.

Now that the above formula is clear I'm going to proceed to another realm. You must choose how you decide to dictate your reality. Does that sound weird? Let me explain. You see, once you have realized that all you have to do is speak in a way that is not in conflict with the laws of karma and universal laws, the sky becomes the limit for what you can accomplish. Let's look at that nexus point. When you have mastered control over your language to the degree that you are effectively neutral because you watch what comes out of your mouth and avoid any karmic pitfalls, you can proceed with the three possible choices for how you conduct yourself from there, or the combination of them that suits your desires most fully. Allow me to explain.

## After Mastering Language…

You see, there are in essence three directions to choose from once control over language is mastered. The first possibility is staying on the straight and narrow path that is karmically neutral, neither pouring karma into the universe nor taking any out. That is definitely the safest bet. That point of view definitely exemplifies the hermetic code of "as above, so below," and one of the powers of the Sphinx: "To conceal", or, as it is also known, "to keep silent". It may even allow for a form of invisibility, as one of my guides tells me. So that's one way you can take it. At best, maybe pulling an Enoch and just vanishing. Poof, gone. At worst, living a colorless existence, which can either be a blessing or not, depending on what you want to accomplish in life. Another way to think of this direction is that it is a very safe path to take. By staying as karmically neutral as possible, we protect ourselves from unseen forces. However, sometimes the most progressive road is also the most dangerous. Conflict is often times the only way things change, and change for the better at that. Consider an egg: it is only through the violent breaking of the egg does the chick hatch.

A caveat to this, though, is that karma is not a "tit for tat" scoring game, but rather a fluidic state of being. By *truly* understanding the underlying principles of the twelve karmic laws, you can improvise more easily for higher quality results. If, as you may recall, "karma" is "consequences", then when we conceive a goal, a desired result, we are choosing to step onto a road where there complete neutrality is impossible; achieving or not achieving that goal is, of course, a consequence. If we understand that karma is fluid, then we can mentally sidestep the polarity perspective of karma, training ourselves to *not* think of karma as "tit for tat." This is a way you can proceed and grow. By being aware that so many things we are exposed to are simply guidelines and states of being, we come into a deeper understanding of our role in this world. This awareness also empowers us to assist others in ways that do not normally come to mind. For example, often people think they can be of assistance if they are constantly offering help, but sometimes the most help we can be comes of being a stable pillar that they can rely on if necessary.

The second approach to take is to just say "I'm going to be me, and to hell with the results." For sure that's a valid point, and, from a magickal perspective, definitely one that would build up the Will necessary to go further in magick. There's just one problem. That attitude breeds the karmic law of attraction. "Like attracts like." If you project that strong ego-willed attitude into the world, you will see that the people that are drawn to you are not necessarily conducive to the growth of your spiritual path. They may be strong willed individuals, but with that lower ego gratification perspective come tests and trials. And, if not controlled properly, that same egotism could lead to arrogance and the bane of most strong-willed people: hubris. Pride is a terrible and subtle pitfall. Be careful that the ego is the higher, more magickal and mystical Will, and not the Will of the lower ego, which operates on desire gratification, and does not advance the evolution of the soul over lifetimes. As it has been said many times throughout the years, the downfall of many a good magician is pride. While I do agree that the above attitude is quite useful and overall healthy, there are too many people that take this to an extreme, which is where the challenges come in. Like any behavior, if it is taken to an extreme and is inflexible, then it becomes a hindrance rather than a blessing.

The third direction is, of course by default, the converse of this drive towards personal desire and gratification. It's the thought "I'm going to come at language from the perspective of pouring love and light into the world." By the law of attraction, you are drawing to you love and light if that's what you are projecting. Isn't that what we all want? Doesn't everyone just want to be happy? It may be a harder road to walk since sometimes it's difficult to love those that, in your mind, may not deserve it, but speaking from a planar perspective it is a higher position to take. Never forget, again, that the higher ground has the advantage, so thus this is a tactical truth as well. The caution that comes with this, though, is that if you're not careful, a serious disconnect between light and being grounded may occur, so it is wise to remain grounded in the physical plane if you choose to pursue this use of language.

At this point it is also wise to mention that pouring light into the world doesn't equate to being blinded or a sucker for those that might use that behavior against you. If there's one thing I've learned about working with the light over the last few decades, it's the fact that if you're really serious about it, the light will burn you, and all it touches. This concept is commonly known as the flames of purification, for things are purified by the light. Another apt parallel for light is that it is the light of clarity, wisdom, and intellect that is issuing forth to dispel the darkness of ignorance. In other words, ignorance is symbolically equated with darkness in a lot of ways, and mental clarity and education with the light. The easiest way to think of this is to understand the most basic of concepts. If we don't know something, then we are "in the dark" about it, and that darkness only lifts when we get educated and clarification on whatever the subject is. However, through mass culture many of us get the message that working with the light is something that is only done by those that work with subtle energies and are looking for a way to handle life. I have noticed that the term "light worker" gets a very bad reputation in a lot of circles because the common thoughtform behind it is that that work is only done by someone that has a bigger heart than brain. I won't get into details about that here, but I believe you get the picture. However, I have discovered that "light workers" exist everywhere, and are not always of that personality type. Some of the most adept light workers that I have encountered have a fine edge to the blade of their intellect that sets them apart from the average person.

Relate this back to vocal magick: if we take this direction with regards to our speaking and conscious creation of our reality, then we should carefully think through what we are supporting and be aware of what to expect as a response from others.

Now that I've addressed the three basic directions, allow me to explain how there are many more directions than the ones I've listed. You see, all three of those can be mixed and matched within any given personal or group paradigm. You could be liberal about your negative language technique, believing that while the stance is "I'm going to be me, and to hell with the results" is the way you want to live your life, you are also open to using other techniques instead of limiting yourself to the absolute implied above. Or you could be love and light with neutrality hidden underneath. See what I mean? It can be as tailor made to you as you choose. Our true Will can be exercised here to construct our individual stories to meet the demands of our individual Will. After all, each day we rewrite our past to find or create situations in which we were the victors.

The approaches to living life are as varied as the colors that are used by artists, so it is wise to remember this as you spiritually develop. There is no cookie cutter mold to follow, but rather life is a constant work in progress. We can blend these three main directions together in any way we see fit, and we can also incorporate other ideas so that we uniquely create our path in a way that reveals to the world who and what we are. There is no reason why we should want to be just like anyone else. After all, it is our free will and uniqueness that sets us apart from other kingdoms of beings on this planet. Individual expression is something to be celebrated and indulged in. The best spiritual system we can use is the one that we most resonate with, and in many cases this is not going to be exactly like anyone or everyone else's. It's going to be a system that uplifts our spirit, and thus perpetuates our spiritual growth. It has been said many times before that all paths lead up to the mountaintop, and this is very true when it comes to spiritual development. The only point to watch out for is that some paths take longer than others, so it is wise to choose the path that is the most expedient, at least if that's what you're into.

It has been my experience that you get farther with sugar than with vinegar, so why would you want to come from any perspective other than exuding love? If, by coming from that perspective, things are a little easier in life, then logically it stands to reason that you would want to do that. Granted, there are problems that come with this stance, and those need to be taken into account as well. For example, a lot of times when someone is coming from that stance of love and light, they can be seen as shallow and superficial, among other not-so-PC adjectives. This is part what I was mentioning above. While this may be true for some it is most definitely not true for all. As with any stereotype, however, it is a stereotype for a reason. I feel that the more people that come from a positive space the better. That is the best way to help out evolution. I elucidated this when I brought up the hundredth monkey syndrome. The more people that use this perspective, the closer we get to reaching a critical mass tipping point in our evolution so that we can evolve away from lower vibrational behaviors. After all, we as a species are no more evolved than the least evolved among us. Often, our words are enough to create change in ourselves and how people perceive us. This also becomes infectious, spreading to those that we encounter. So, in short, all is well when operating from that stance. It may be more of a challenge, but it is definitely the brightest of the three basic stances. Approaching life from this perspective also sets you apart from the average person that approaches life from a fear-based perspective, so you may find that what you believe and live is in conflict with many people. That's okay, but sometimes it requires a psychological adjustment.

Now let me address the contradictory stance. It, too, has a strong case. Just hear it out, but if you're paying attention, you'll see the problems with it. "I'm going to be me, and to hell with the results." All right, let's look at this. It implies that the individual's way is right, at least for them. And they feel strongly enough about it that they would adhere to that set of principles doggedly enough to put it in those terms. It also shows a lack of respect for anyone else, and lack of concern for karma. While there may be some people out there that don't believe in karma, karma believes in us all. This is a voice coming from a lower vibratory stance, one of gratification on the earth plane only, with very little understanding or concern for any of the other planes. It is also very arrogant, confrontational, and angry. A lot of times it is associated with the "When you're dead, you're dead" belief. Perhaps they have an understanding of the astral plane on a subconscious level, since their worldview is very much motivated by emotion. Emotion is what builds the astral plane, so it stands to reason that they are working with the astral because their attitude is definitely charged with emotions. The key, however, is that there is no logic in the above viewpoint. By consciously watching what you say, you are coming at reality from a logic-based stance, and logic is associated with the mental plane, which rules the astral[19]. A good alternative to that view that would achieve karmically better results would be something similar to "I'm going to live my life the way I choose to, because I know that "Pure Will, unassuaged of purpose, delivered from the lust of result, is every way perfect.[20]"

---

[19] Dion Fortune, The Circuit of Force, is dedicated to the direction energy flows among the planes.
[20] Aleister Crowley, The Book of the Law, chapter 1, verse 44 (I:44).

How does the above statement apply to the above viewpoint "I'm going to be me, and to hell with the results"? That's simple. By knowing that your Will is pure, then you also know that karmically speaking everything is sound, and the consequences will not constrain you from your personal growth. The trick is differentiating between your ego-centered will, and the will of your "soul" (Or oversoul, or holy guardian Angel, or HGA, or etc.).

I spent a long time living life from that perspective, and I loved every minute of it. It is good to not let others dictate your mental state. However, it shows a lack of willingness to cooperate with others, and it also shows closed-mindedness.

To be ignorant of one's true Will is far more common than not, and sometimes that's a leading inhibiter of achieving the beauties of life. In this book, I offer one beginning technique to achieve knowing your "true self". Once you gain control of your language, you will quickly see how easy it becomes to create your reality, and how you can use this mastery towards knowing your True Will. The True Will is that concept that we fundamentally know we are here to execute during this lifetime. Sometimes it's easy to discover, and sometimes it's hard, but regardless, it is something that is of the utmost importance to work with.

### Reincarnation and the True Self

After working with language control for an extended period of time it will become apparent that the Akashic Records are not that hard to access, and through that knowledge can be found a more personal and intimate tool for conversing with your True Self[21], on a more regular basis. The Akashic Records are the records of the soul, so

---

[21] At this point, I'm going to use "True Self" instead of HGA, group soul, or whatever term one may use. They are all the same, after all.

to speak. In the Akashic Records is contained a full accounting of what our individual souls have experienced. Thus, they are subjective to each person, but it has also been said that there is an Akashic Record that covers the whole of humanity. The term "Akashic" is a derivative of the word "Akasha," which translates to "aethyr" from its native tongue of Sanskrit. Thus the Akashic Records are the records of Spirit, or it could be seen that they are spirit records. In either case, they are something that an individual can tap into that gives access to information from past and future lives, and this can be very useful for our overall spiritual growth. There are many different ways to access them, but the predominant way is through hypnotic regression.

The True Self is not as elusive as one may perceive. I hear people say all the time that it is a special occurrence when they talk to the True Self, or that it is a challenge to talk to the True Self. I don't discount where they are coming from when they say that, but I do have to wonder why they have installed those roadblocks in their spiritual growth. The True Self is simply the "True Self". I can't think of any other way to describe it. It is the best of what we are in this lifetime, and through accumulated lifetimes. It is what we strive to manifest in our lifetimes when it decides to come down into physical form as what we commonly know as "us". In esoteric teachings, who we are on this third dimensional plane is known as the personality self, and fleeting when put into context of the passage of time in the grand scheme of things. The True Self is what endures through the aeons. The True Self is the culminated best of all lifetimes. Seeing that, why is it so hard to know the Will of the True Self? Could it just be as simple as fear or self-doubt? Often times the True Self is seen as nebulous, when in reality it is something that can be accessed when we take the time to still the mind and go within for greater insight and clarity. When we go into the inner world, we put ourselves in a position to grow on the finer planes, and this radiates out to our day-to-day life. By choosing to do our best each and every day, we are making the statement to the everyday world that we will do the very most we can with the tools at our disposal.

Here's a short side note, but a necessary one. In the interaction of the planes, there is no such thing as time. Thoughts, words, and gears being put into motion all occur at a different rate of manifestation than what we are familiar with here on the third dimensional plane. And, as the Kybalion addresses, the Hindus teach, and the book *Power vs. Force* clarifies, the structure of the multiverse[22] is vibration. Everything is made of varying degrees of vibrations. Having clarified where I'm coming from, let us return to our previously scheduled discussion.

If, then, vibrations are the basis of the multiverse, it stands to reason that the best way to affect change is by tapping into those vibrations and altering them to your Will. This is the basic concept for Mantras. Mantras are an ancient system that uses different vibrations, strung together syllabically, to affect change in a particular area of the human condition. For more information on mantras, look into the author Thomas Ashley-Farrand, one of the leading experts in the west on the subject, and a really great guy to boot!

You can use your everyday language in a similar fashion to mantras to achieve results that are just as potent. The main difference between mastering mantras, and the form of mastering language that I'm addressing here, is that mantras are more precise, while mastering your native tongue is broader. Allow me to explain. If you do a mantra to bring prosperity into your life, then that is exactly what will happen in the time and manner it is meant to manifest. However, if you have a mastery of language, you

---

[22] Universe is the common term. I prefer multiverse because there is more than one universe out there, all happening concurrently.

can address the karmic issues that affect you with regards to prosperity. If you wanted to address those karmic issues with a mantra, there is a separate mantra for that purpose. Mantras are the scalpel, while language mastery is the knife.

Another difference between the two is that the theory of a mantra is based on manipulation of the chakra petals, and mastery of language is not. The chakras are interdimensional energy vortexes that exist in the human energy field and body, running through the central meridian of form. Each one has petals on it, like a flower, and when they are manipulated a particular way they can produce very potent and healing results. When you do mantras, it usually involves setting aside time and focusing on the mantras. When you use mastery of language, it doesn't involve setting aside any time whatsoever. All it takes is awareness and conscious control. Therefore, it is a more versatile tool, although mantras are more potent in the short term and when properly applied to their very specific purposes.

I clarify both tools to show that there are different ways to affect the foundation vibrations of the multiverse. Why do I clarify this? Since there is no time among the other realms, the best way to reach those other realms, and beings in those realms, is through, among other ways, vibratory control. Once you are aware and in control of the language that comes out of your mouth, you can then guide it to project whatever you choose into the multiverse. Pondering time and how to use it, we put ourselves in a greater position of control over it. For example, everyone only gets twenty-four hours in a day, so we're all on the same page with that, but some people cover a lot of ground during that time, while others don't. By living an abundant and aware life, we empower ourselves further than if we were just lazy about it.

Here's an illustration to clarify. If you were having a rough time in your life and you wanted to make sure that all the obstacles in your way were being removed, or at least minimized, you could do mantras to the Hindu deity Ganesh who is the remover of obstacles. Or you could simply say, through casual conversation with someone, something to the effect of "Yeah, like I'll have a hard road to walk! Yeah, right." Trust me, it has been my personal experience that both achieve the end result of removing obstacles. The only thing that differs is the method used and other details. Because of his power over removing obstacles, Ganesh is also helpful in changing consciousness, since sometimes obstacles drop away once your perspective is changed. Something additional that differentiates the two is that, by using language mastery in the above way, you are doing more karmic manipulation than you do if you say mantras to Ganesh. Additionally, if you are using mantras to Ganesh, you are also manipulating the chakras. With language mastery you are not. With language mastery, you are kicking a door open by allowing almost anything to help you with your current project. I'm sure that idea scares some of you, but the author has no fear of that. "Fear", like Frank Herbert stated in his novel *Dune,* "is the mind killer". This stance is also echoed in Aleister Crowley's *The Book of the Law,* and other religious texts throughout the last one hundred years or so. Of course there are other differences between the two methods, but I feel these are enough to illustrate my point.

The concept of affirmations may come to mind here as well, but I will return to them later in this book. Suffice to say for now that they are repetitive patterns of speech and thought that can be used to powerful effects.

In closing this chapter out, I would like to mention one final thought on why you should come from a stance of love when mastering language. Love is the highest vibration known. It can take you higher than anything else, faster than any other way. Love is the highest vibration where we are because we are a second ray solar system in the seven rays system[23], and the second ray is the ray of love and compassion. Astrologically, it would correspond to Venus. There are other rays, though, for the curious readers to ponder. Yes, this also means that in other systems where there is sentient life, an energy other than love would be the highest energy to work with. Yes, this does assume that you believe in life in other parts of the cosmos, but I feel confident that if you're reading this, you already have that belief.

However, a word of warning and of forethought must be mentioned here. Love is not ignorance personified. Love is not fear. Love is not control. Love is a living current of energy that can be tapped into and used, but, like any other energetic pattern, must be treated with care and respect, for too much of a good thing can turn the core of the pomegranate rotten. My mind is drawn to such psychological malaise as abuse, addiction, and codependency. Those issues can come from a misunderstanding and or a misuse of love just as fast as love can help manifestation. By being in control of language, you can defend against such pitfalls through awareness. Awareness is the true secret key to creating your reality. By raising your vibration to that of the highest, which is love, you are also raising your consciousness and through effect, those around you, if only on a subconscious level.

This is commonly known as living from a blending of the heart and the mind, and has grown in popularity in recent years. As a good friend of mine always said: "Soft hearted does not mean soft headed!" There is a common misconception that people that have a big heart are

---

[23] The seven ray system is a system of teachings that comes from India, which has been extensively developed through Theosophy. In short, it states that there are seven colors of light that emanate out from the source. Each color has correspondences, properties, and concepts associated with it.

gullible, and this doesn't have to be the case. By using logic and intelligence, a successful blend can occur that can produce impressive effects. Awareness is the first step to overcoming the separation of the intuition and the mind. By being aware and in conscious control over what we're projecting in our lives, we come into greater alignment with living our True Will, and thus we achieve more growth. By being proactive in our approach with this, we take the stance that we are the ones that create our lives, we are not the victims of circumstance, nor are we simply tossed about on the winds of change to be blown through an ocean of chaos. Many ancient religions taught that life and civilization arose out of the primordial sea of chaos, so it doesn't make sense to return to that primordial state. Organizing and ordering things in our day to day paradigm is something that can produce great results, but with this approach also comes greater responsibility and harder work, so it's not for the lazy; it's for the victor and the aggressor.

# Chapter 7
# Colorize It!

In the previous chapter I discussed the space to come from when learning mastery of language. In this chapter I'm going to explain the potency of metaphors and how to provide color to your created reality. It is one thing to simply be in control of your language to the point that you've mastered what you are projecting into the multiverse and how to achieve the results you choose. It is another thing entirely to do this with style and flair. By colorizing our speech, we turn our conversations into 3D experiences. Of course this is something we want to prepare ourselves for extensively before we engage in it, but all of us eventually make our conversations more immersive by putting our personality self-projection into them. Through this technique we can tap into the part of our mind that works with subjects such as art, the opera, and many other liberal arts. These are also means of communication through vibration, remember, whether by the addition of more layers of sound through music or the use of the vibrations we call light. Up until now the subject of language mastery has been a very direct and heavy subject, so let's lighten it up a little bit!

This chapter is going to show you how you can spice things up a little. What good is it to go around with a mastery of language if it is seen as a challenge, or, even worse, as boring? That seems pretty silly to me. Therefore in this chapter I'm going to extrapolate on a previously mentioned method of talking generically. Speaking karmically neutrally, as mentioned before, is a method that can be very valuable, but at the same time it can be highly limiting because it doesn't lend itself very easily to personalization. If everyone spoke very matter-of-factly, it would make the world a very different place than it is now, for we would all be androgynous, as would our cultures. The homogenization of culture is something that has been a popular topic over the last few years in many different areas of life, so I won't get into details here. However, I will use my standard response of "you'll find plenty of books on the subject if you do your research."

If you speak with this sort of generality, you can access more Akashic Records information than if you don't use this technique. By using phrases like "my chariot" instead of "my car," you open yourself up to more timeless memories. Now I'm going to expand on that. It is one thing to speak broadly in order to produce those results. It is another thing entirely to speak with confidence in a colorful manner to produce those same results, if not better ones. The true key to that is the concept of a metaphor. According to Webster's Dictionary, the definition of a metaphor is: "a figure of speech in which a word or phrase literally denoting one kind of object or idea is used in place of another to suggest a likeness or analogy between them (as in *drowning in money*)[24]. I choose to make this clear as quartz right now because I'm going to a new realm. We've established up until this point why one should strive to come from a place of love when delivering speech, and how time-neutral terms can be a key to accessing the Akashic Records. Now we are following the White Whale into new, unknown depths. This chapter is going to address the very powerful technique of using metaphors to affect mental change, thus gaining control over one's mind.

What does this have to do with language, you ask? If language is reality, then I am going to construct my reality to my liking. Therefore, the next question becomes "how do I achieve this"? It took me a few years to realize and

---

[24] http://www.webster.com/dictionary/metaphor

gain control over my speech enough that I could do it, but it has brought me much success since mastering it.

A large part of my path is Egyptian Magick. So the first thing I did to access not only past lives from there, but also to feel more happy in general, was to begin using terms that meant something in ancient Khem, and what they would represent in this day and age.

So, for example, when asking for a piece of paper, I would instead ask for a piece of papyrus. Of course whenever I did that, I got stares all the time, and usually I had to repeat myself in the common tongue, but I did not do that technique *forever*! I only used that technique long enough to open a channel to the Akashic Records relating to ancient Khem. This became a channel that I could go to and access at any time, with relative ease. As soon as that relationship was established, I quit being so goofy! The technique had been tried. The link and the access had been created with proof that could be quantified and justified, so therefore the technique was recorded as a success. Now I could move on to step 2.

Step 2: After mastering the mental association, and re-routing my thought patterns (in essence; Think about it), I then began applying what I had learned. Here's how I proceeded: Now that it had been established that I could draw on those Akashic Records at will, I began looking at common manners of speech, and then took that process regional. How people speak in St. Louis, Missouri is very different than the way they speak on the East Coast, for example. But it's not only accents. It is also the way sentences are put together, and what (you guessed it) metaphors they use to describe situations and people in their lives. Allow me to extrapolate on that. I lived in Ohio for two years and when I was there, I discovered that they used different slang and metaphors than what I was used to in St. Louis. Now I realize that this concept has been known for centuries, and when I realized it, I realized also that I knew that, but had forgotten it from lack of use. It was no revelation, but by having that brought into the forefront of my consciousness it brought my focus to it. When I looked at what I had rediscovered, I sought to see how I could use that magickally. This realization and subsequent practice with, unleashed a potency that surprised even me! Here's a sample: If a normal metaphoric cliché is: "Cheap as dirt, then I would change it to be: "Cheap as two bits of copper".

The first few times that I did this, I felt awkward, but after a few months of changing things around a bit with different clichés and situations, I eventually adjusted my language to my taste. I went from the above statement to something subtler. And from there I went to something even more subtle, and also more intelligent. I kept playing with combinations of what I wanted in my paradigm and what I didn't until I found myself the happiest. With regards to the above metaphor, I changed it to "Cheap as two bits". It is my experience that most people know what the phrase "two bits" means, and by leaving the word "copper" off, it was subtler, so it went to my audience's subconscious more quickly. This not only sticks with the target audience longer, but it also has a greater impact. In the above example, by using "two bits" in that way I showed that I was well read enough to speak like that with confidence. So for the most part it is a very positive technique.

The draw back to this is that, by leaving the word "copper" off, I did open the door to miscommunication, but that can be dealt with using additional skill and refinement. In this case though, the door that was opened was only opened a crack, as for all practical purposes the meaning of the phrase changed very little. There are plenty of instances, though, where leaving off a word can have drastic consequences, and so changes should be made judiciously and with careful consideration of potential consequences.

Once I had completed this sequence of transformations, I knew that my experiment had been a success, which I knew that it would be all along. You could, to a certain extent, control your happiness by controlling your language. As I felt happier, I could more easily come at things from a more loving perspective. Thus I could affect positive change in my life, as opposed to instigating change with no control over how it might affect me. When I realized this, I also saw the almost unlimited potential that was available to me to shape not only my reality, but the reality of those whom I came into contact with. With this realization came a sense of empowerment that I had not experienced before, and it felt wonderful!

I've got this down to the point now that I can strategically place metaphors in conversations so that I use the fewest metaphors possible for maximum effect. After I realized that I had this technique down to that level of detail, I knew I could move forward. And I was happier overall. I owed it all to control over language, and what that truly means. Once the mastery was rote, I began working on delivery and strategic placement in conversation, thus turning it into an art form, rather than approaching it as a scientist might view a subject infected with an artificially placed virus. As the good book says: "The Method of Science, the aim of religion"[25]. Now I could move forward putting my own coloring onto the majority produced paradigm that passes for reality in America in 2014! One of the most rewarding things one can do is to decide how they want to paint the consensual mural of this paradigm that we all live in. Most people are content to go through life almost subconsciously, drifting along, and knowing only the fulfillment of base desires. However, if you're reading this book then I know that you

[25] Crowley, Aleister. *The Equinox*, volume 1, number 1; frontispiece.

are interested in taking an active hand in painting that consensual mural we all experience in a way that is unique to you. While yes, part of this has to do with considering what we have to contribute to society, part of it also has to do with what kind of legacy we choose to leave behind.

When the art of the metaphor is mastered, true bending of the fabric of reality can begin on a whole new level. By governing speech, you can train people to associate a given thought pattern with you or a particular idea in general. At this point it is a good idea to begin looking into colors and color energy[26]. For example, the color red is primarily associated with force and activity. Therefore, if you used the word red, or metaphors based on that particular color, or attributes of that color in your metaphors, it will train people on a subconscious level to think of you as a very active, energetic person. This is nice when dealing with people who believe differently than you do. When I'm around my immediate blood family, I choose my words carefully because I know that all paths are inherently the same, and all lead to the godhead, but we all have different belief systems. They do not share the path I'm on, but I love them, and I see many commonalities in beliefs when I talk to them. So I use more spiritually centered words as opposed to words focused on my path specifically or their religion, so that our commonality is demonstrated to them on a subtle level, and I shape what they see and know of me. This keeps me oriented from a light perspective and trains me to be as tolerant and open-minded as possible. This training of myself instills the discipline necessary to keep my awareness at its peak operating level. At this peak level I keep control over my reality, and my mind is always brought back to building it, so that not only do I create my

---

[26] Three excellent books on the topic are: How to Heal with Colors by Ted Andrews, Color Magic for Beginners by Richard Webster, and 7 Days of Magick by Ellen Dugan; all from Llewellyn.

reality, I am also happier overall. By being happier, I have more to give, and feel more comfortable giving.

When developing your means of presentation to others, remember that clothing should be considered as well. To begin with, it is the color of the clothes that matter more than the price tag. Color coordination with the days of the week is a highly underrated magickal tool. Traditional correspondences with the days of the week are: Sunday-Yellow and/or Gold; Monday-Silver, Light Blue, Light Gray; Tuesday-Red; Wednesday-Orange, Yellow; Thursday-Purple and Royal Blue; Friday-Green, Pink, Pastels; Saturday-Black. Used in conjunction with color-based language focused on the particular days of the week, clothing can be instrumental in projecting a certain mindset. To illustrate, consider this: If you wear predominantly black clothes, but your language reflects a much more vibrant personality, what do you think will be remembered of you after a conversation? It has been my experience that the memories will be blander than if the two (colors of wardrobe and colors of language) are working in unison and harmony. This doesn't necessarily mean that the color of language and of clothing has to be the same, but rather, they should be complimentary. You could wear red clothes, and speak in words like "sunny", "bright", "optimistic", and other bright adjectives, that would encourage and enhance that entire current of energy. Through portrayal of that whole picture can an accurate picture be painted, in accord to one's Will. In today's society people are more and more becoming visual learners, and because of this what we visually project is mattering more and more. Light is also a form of vibration, and thus a medium that communicates.

## Mental Clarity and Focus

Metaphors are a lot like Mudras. Both are underrated, and both are not commonly practiced or known techniques, but both have exceptional potency when done right and done often. Language is a way of orally expressing and calling on currents of energy that can be used to one's benefit. Mudras are a way of guiding, among other things, pranic flow, and calling upon a current of energy for a desired result. Language does the same thing, only it is more of a direct route to creation because you can do it without any out of the ordinary mannerisms. And, talking is done a lot more than just hand gestures, no matter what some road ragers will tell you!

I know many, many people that use metaphors to be colorful and to show their own inner uniqueness, and often times they are some of the most alive and vibrant people that I know. They are generally some of the most creative as well. The challenge that comes with the use of metaphors, though, is that if your audience isn't in line with this particular approach, the use of metaphors actually makes things worse. If you are using a metaphor for something and your audience is a direct, down to earth person, then not only might the metaphor not work, but it also may work against you. This is something to be mindful of when dealing with social institutions. Of course the obvious way around this issue is to be mindful of who you are speaking to, and to adjust your communication style appropriately. In a way, this brings us full circle to what we discussed earlier about the "I'm living life my way" approach. I believe it is clear how these two ideas come together, but let me clarify. If someone takes that self-centered attitude and they use a lot of metaphors on a regular basis, they are creating many issues for themselves by not adjusting their communication style to their audience. In other words, appropriateness is the key to unlocking successful navigation of the world.

## Deprogramming and Regaining Control

Anyway, back to the topic. Language is one of the most powerful magickal tools at your disposal. It has the capacity for a large variety of uses, and is malleable to what job needs done. If you want to test your growth on language control, then just watch a movie or a television show. You'll hear people talk all the time, and when your awareness includes being aware of your own language, you'll hear things come out of the mouths of people in the media, and you can almost cringe at what is being thrown out into the universe so casually. Cringe, or smile at it. I don't watch a lot of television, but when I do, it's usually done under a magnifying glass, looking to see what is being poured into the astral plane. Part of this is due to my extensive media background, but part of it also has to do with me wanting to be aware of what is being pumped into my brain. I want to know what astral thought forms are being fed to the mass populace of humanity. Since the predominant television programming is aimed at tugging at the heartstrings, then I know what general emotion is getting fed. Most of the programs on television are predicated around the emotions, and the rare exceptions to this are primarily the ones that are educational, and thus address the mental plane. Emotional manipulation is something that the powers that be are very adept at, and because of this, it is wise for each and every one of us to be ever vigilant and on guard against things that may otherwise manipulate us in unhealthy ways.

For example, if you watch television for a week during the normal programming hours, and you notice a pattern of, say, crime shows, then the level of reality that is being fed is two fold. The first is the astral, because normally there is hurt, pride, or any other number of emotions that fuel the crimes being solved. That means that those entities that feed on those negative emotions are being fed.

But on the bright side, it also means that the mental plane is being fed, because it is usually logic and deduction that is being promoted as an answer to the very lower astral energies that commit the crimes. Greed, rage, jealousy, and pride are all countered by logic and deduction. Subconsciously logic is being promoted as an answer to base knee jerk reactions and consequences. Is this part of the media masters' programming when they design their shows and their marketing strategies? Of course it is. But it is only a reaction to what the masses of humanity are asking for in their "entertainment". Sometimes the intent of those same people and organizations is to control the people by keeping them distracted and divided, though, so it is wise to analyze each situation as it comes up.

Once you get an eye for watching what other people say, then naturally the next step is to take a hard look at yourself. If negative people surround you all day long, then maybe too much negativity is being projected, and a simple language readjustment will take care of the problem. At the very least it would set an example, maybe not a conscious example, but an example nonetheless. If you are less negative, taking leadership by example, then those around you will be less negative, or you will vibrate away from them, as mentioned earlier. Half of the time they won't know that they are being affected by you in this way, but you'll be aware since you were the instigator of the transformation. It may take awhile to get the ball rolling regarding finding your groove, but when it begins, its impact on your immediate environment will become evident.

When this level of observation and commitment is realized, you will quickly realize that life itself is a lot easier than you are conditioned to believing. There are some people that would counter that this is all a complex way of saying that the more positive one is, the better life is. Yes, this is true. There's no denying that. But, now that language has been looked at from several different angles, using several techniques on several subjects, it should be clear that I'm not countering that claim. All I'm doing is providing tools that one can use to one's benefit.

People that say I'm making something overly complicated aren't seeing the bigger picture. True, if you stay positive and optimistic, things will go well for you. However, if you learn control over your language, you are staying positive and optimistic, **and** you are staying that way from a reasonable, logical, rational stance. In short, you are arriving at the same conclusion, but coming at it *from above!* I don't know about you, but if someone asks me to take something on blind faith, I question it. I question it until the cows come home. I've got to know what my intuition is telling me, so I have to have answers to every single question I have. My mind is very active, so I have a lot of questions. Those that tell you to simply keep your chin up, stay optimistic, and positive, are basically asking you to put faith in what they are telling you.

I don't know about you, but the last time I checked I had a physical form. The person telling me that opinion most likely has physical form, or is created by someone that has physical form. Guess what? That makes us both capable of error. To control a plane, you must come down on it from above, as per the guidelines set down in Dion Fortune's book *The Circuit of Force*. You don't gain control of a plane by coming at it from the level of that plane. The circuit of force flows better and stronger if you come at it from above. I agree that we should stay positive and optimistic, but I believe that is true because of the karmic law that you draw to you what you project. I don't believe what someone who is flesh and blood like me tells me unless it resonates with me. If it doesn't resonate with me, then I look inward to myself to find out why. I believe it because I control my reality. I'm not buying what they're selling. I'm not giving away my personal power!

All of the things that I've discussed in this chapter can be applied to take your language control to the next level in a way that is tailor made to you, and is not rote, but rather dynamic. By adding things like color and metaphor, we put ourselves in a position to make our own statement on reality, which is very effective for making an impression and getting people to listen to us and remember us long past leaving their presence. Another useful technique beyond metaphors is the allegory, so let us take a moment to discuss these.

## Allegories

Allegories are stories that are symbolic in nature, and are usually used to convey a particular point. An excellent example of this is Aesop's Fables. The thinker Plato also made extensive use of this technique in a lot of his later writings. Often this technique is used because if the author was direct about something it could get them into trouble with the law or the government. Because of this, a lot of social commentary is done in an allegorical fashion.

I use allegories extensively when teaching because it keeps the interest of the audience. Sometimes people don't understand what you're telling them until you use a story to convey it. People can usually relate to the characters in the story, especially when they see a reflection of themselves in it, thus making the message easier to digest. One of the points to be aware of when it comes to allegories is that the type of allegory used dictates how it is received. For example, you may have a point that you want to convey, and it can be conveyed either through a soft, gentle story, or a horror story. Sometimes it is wise to use the approach that is most appropriate to the audience that you're writing for so as to raise a sympathetic reaction, but other times you may find it wiser to use the allegory that produces the most shock value. As with metaphors, though, discernment should be practiced when you choose your allegorical style, so that you do not run into situations where you may find the narrative funny and interesting, but your audience does not.

Allegories should be used very carefully, though, as the type of allegories that we use determines how others think we see the world. For example, if we use nothing but horrific allegories, then our audience may think that we are full of that kind of energy, when in our minds we are simply being playful. When the only thing that someone has to go on about us is what we say, then to a certain extent our hands are tied. We can of course ignore this piece of wisdom, but I have seen time and again that if we ignore it, we are intentionally short-circuiting our own personal power in the name of laziness and self-centeredness.

When you choose to work with allegories, it is also wise to remember to use allegories that your audience will understand more than ones you are comfortable with. I don't use the same allegories when I'm overseas that I use when I'm in the States. I also don't use the same allegories in the country that I use in the city. One of the implications of this is that studying different regions and cultures is essential so that we are not caught off guard when it comes to using allegories in the proper context. Studying different cultures can provide great stimulation, and help us better learn the modern world that we live in. When we work with this technique, an increase in vocabulary occurs. I am a strong believer in the building of the vocabulary. Only through constantly adding words do we increase our accuracy with language. By increasing our accuracy with language, we put ourselves in a position to manifest in a clearer way. Through this clarity, things come more clearly into focus, and we can fine tune what our life will contain. We also alleviate any existing grey issues that could be troublesome if left unattended. Yes, life is a sliding scale of grey, but we have control over the grey areas of our lives to a large extent, and we would be wise to remember this.

Allegories and metaphors are two very potent techniques to use, but both have the prerequisite of appropriateness and discretion. Only by paying attention *when* we use them do we gain social graces that we may not use if we are not familiar with these tools. When this is accomplished, we can blend into almost any group in society, in some ways performing a disappearing act, and in other ways, becoming the perfect chameleon. The third piece to the puzzle is adjectives. Adjectives are, as we noted before, words that modify nouns, so a lot of times they add detail and color to whatever it is that we are conveying. A lot of people use adjectives to convey emotions and subjective perspective, but adjectives can also be used to show perception and an eye for detail. If carefully used, adjectives can provide great clarification on any given subject. Through the careful use of adjectives, we can provide detail in our speech that can make things clear to our audience. However, if we don't pay attention to our adjectives, we may tip our hand to how we perceive things, and thus we may want to think twice before using them. I personally use adjectives that are more focused on revealing details rather than conveying my subjective opinion on something. The main reason for using them is to be as accurate in my speech as possible. If you work with adjectives, you also discover that your attention to sentence structure and grammar is also increased, as the proper insertion of adjectives is paramount to clarity and competent language demonstration.

When all three of these techniques are remembered, we have a full palette to work with when it comes to creating and illuminating our reality using language. Any combination of the three can be used, as despite being distinct techniques they can easily be blended together for greater effect. It is important to keep in mind that using any of them does change the psychological perspective of the communicator, as it draws the attention to focus and clarity. By knowing when to use such tools and when not to, we increase our ability to move through the necessary sections of society in order to manifest our true Will on this physical plane. I find all of this fairly funny because being mindful of this takes me back to English classes I had when I was a young boy. It has always made me smile when I find that magical teachings take me back to school and my formative years. I enjoy realizing that some of the most profound truths have been there all along, hiding in plain sight.

# Chapter 8
# Details are the Sign of an Alert Mind

For the next few pages, we are going to be discussing the very important aspect of precision. The choice to be as precise as possible in speech is a very wise and correct choice. When describing something to someone, be as precise as you can be. Why? First of all, it sharpens the metaphors that are building blocks for your reality. Secondly, it trains your mind to be as astute as possible, which opens the door to magickal experiences. Third, it sharpens the memory. If you record your experiences in your magickal diary you can then review them later to see what colors, patterns, and other things have followed you, and when.

Consider the following scenario: Let's say that after reflecting in your magickal diary you realize that during waning moons you not only tend to be a little more depressed but also notice yourself using a the color red often in your descriptions to other people when you construct a metaphor. Going by the color wheel, you consciously choose to put the opposite color in your metaphors and wardrobe, so you decide to add greens. After three months, you notice that now on waning moons, you're not as depressed as you were. When you achieve a level of awareness that lets you put the diary down and remain conscious of this on a moment-by-moment basis, the true potency of language control will hit you. It is the framework within which we work to create our reality. The vibrations that emerge from our lips every day are just as vital as having and following a moral code!

A theory that I put forth is simple, and based on ancient principles. At the base of the Qabalistic Tree of Life is Malkuth. For those of you that aren't familiar with the

Qabalistic Tree of Life, in essence it is a universal filing cabinet where all of our experiences can be filed and correlated for reflection, and is at its heart a method of parceling out the divine so that it is easier to understand, digest, and work with. The underlying concept is that the godhead is too big to understand as one subject, so it is broken down into ten aspects and twenty-two ways of behavior or thought that bind those ten points together. The point of Malkuth relates to the physical world and physical manifestations, which are the most condensed point of divinity.

When we speak, the vibrations that come out of our mouths are of a lower vibration than when it is still a thought. Therefore the lower vibration is more in tune with the vibrations of the "physical" plane we interact with every day. Since it is more in tune, it effects change more quickly. But, it also takes the longest to enact. You always have conscious control over what you say. When a thought occurs to you, you have to then put it into words before you vocalize it. I know that some people are thinking that they are guilty of speaking before thinking, but I dare them to challenge that perception of themselves. Here's a technique to try. Before any word comes out of your mouth, every day, slow your instincts down and review in your head what you are planning to say. Then, if you choose, voice it. Gain control over your mind to the degree that you can think about something at least a split second before voicing it. This will encourage the mind to study the power of the moment. I believe that you would be very impressed with the results after using that technique for two or three months.

Operating on the converse of this, when operating with more Kether-centered ideas at the top of the Qabalistic Tree of Life, the vibration should be higher to match. Kether is a much higher vibration, and therefore more centered on non-voiced thoughts. Thoughts more focused on love and higher vibrational ideas are better suited for raising internal vibrations. It's not that there's anything wrong if you don't use higher vibrational energetics to achieve higher vibrational manifestations. It's just that by using those energetics it makes the road easier. Saying that you will use those energetics and actually using them, however, are two different things entirely. That comes down to a question of personal integrity.

As a side note, it is wise to remember a teaching from Theosophy, which is that "thought begets form." As we think, we create our reality and bring into being beliefs and concepts that float through our heads on a minute-to-minute basis. Energetically, this teaching tells us that we receive messages from spirit in our minds, and that is faster than speech. Thus, speech is a lower vibration than thought, more condensed and closer to the material. Thus the more that we work with thought control, the closer we are to spirit, which means that our vibration is higher, and the subtle realms become more accessible. One of the ways that we can work with this is to control our thoughts, obviously, but also to control our speech so that we are training ourselves to be mindful and to control our thoughts from the other direction. Of course both speech and thought control are important to work with, but focusing on one can feed the other. This also means that if you choose to work on neither, then you are displaying sloppiness. Another point to be aware of here is that symbols are of a higher vibration than words, and are the language of the subconscious. Symbols bypass the conscious mind, and when this occurs, greater information can be conveyed in a faster and more direct manner. This is one of the foundations for art as a medium of communication.

Anyway, back to our point. Now that we have explored combining color coordination and moods with language, we will expand on that concept. Every day that you are out in public and interacting with another being is a communication between divinity and you. If you are going through your workday and you notice that the people you work with are mostly wearing red, then there is a message there. Unless the people coordinated their outfits intentionally or there is an occasion for the colors, then there is something deeper and subtler going on. A lot of times that color is coming up for a reason. Here's an example:

Let's say that your current work environment is under a lot of stress due to deadlines. It would be no surprise then, if a lot of people were wearing red during that time, since red is associated with activity and energy. Even purple could be easily understood, sine purple is a color associated with ceremony and order, and sometimes the best way to do something is to do it ceremonially to bring things in line with order. I had a job in higher education for awhile and over the course of a few months I noticed that a lot of the people that got along very well usually dressed in the same color shirt on certain days. We actually had a discussion about that, and it came to light that we didn't plan it, but rather it just subconsciously happened. I also later discovered that all of us had similar astrological components in our charts. Often, through the karmic law of attraction, we end up in situations like this. Some could say that this is a minor form of telepathy, but whatever the cause, it is worth noting because it shows how auric fields blend, and how we are influenced by the people we spend a substantial amount of time around in our immediate environment.

However, if there is nothing going on in the workplace that would explain certain colors being worn, then a deeper meaning should be considered. If the workplace is currently a place of serenity and peace and a lot of the color red was being worn, then a more esoteric meaning should be sought. What day of the week is it? Is it a Tuesday, whose color is red? If not, then what? What message is spirit trying to convey to you through showing you red in such a quantity? To me, that's where the fun starts, because from that point forward it's all in the research!

Making this observation in life will train the mind to a new level of awareness. If you can train your mind to see this sort of interplay between you and divinity, then you can easily train yourself to be conscious of language, since language is of a lower vibration than color recognition. You also open yourself up to a greater dialogue with your subconscious mind, the universe, and all of those that you encounter. As the old saying goes, "a picture is worth a thousand words," and this is especially true of symbolism, both personal and universal.

Colors are one of the best ways to reach the subconscious, both the subconscious of you and others. This has been an idea that has been around for years and is commonly used in art, particularly as the "flashing color" concept. This can also be very useful for helping you step out onto the astral plane. I strongly encourage you to research flashing colors and how they can assist in astral work, and how they affect the mind in general. Suffice for now, though, that it is enough to be aware of the fact that colors can affect the mind in very subtle yet powerful ways.

## Breath

Next we will touch briefly on the science of breath. I'm not going to go into great detail about it here, as once again there are many, many books that can address the subject in detail. It is my intent to give you a brief overview of what is out there in case you're not familiar with them. Much of our treatment of the science of breath, as it is known, comes from eastern traditions such as Hinduism and has been around for centuries. It is a massive body of work to study, but definitely worth it, even if you only touch on basic concepts.

If you practice the science of breath, then you know how much potency is available to you through use of these techniques. By controlling your breath you are, in essence, controlling the flow of energy into and out of your body. In Hindu thought, prana is the essence of life, and it is carried on sunlight and in the air we breathe. Therefore, when we are controlling and manipulating our breath, we are working with prana, or the essence of life, directly. This is particularly of note when considering how it impacts your language. How does it impact language, you ask? Allow me to explain.

By studying the science of breath[27], you are studying a technique that is applied to the mouth and nose. The control over breath that comes through practicing such techniques subconsciously impacts your speech, in addition, of course, to the skill it provides at controlling the energy that your speech carries. I have a friend that is a Zen Buddhist, and while we've never talked about the subject, I have noticed that he is more conscious of his speech than most. Granted, it may take him a little longer to get his point across because he's choosing his words carefully, but I am good with that. I know too many people who talk to hear themselves talk, or who talk at such a fast pace that they basically are not thinking before talking, and that, to me, is a greater sin than talking slowly. However, it is worth mentioning here that sometimes people use fast speech to pull a con job, but usually a well tuned intuition can bring clarity to who is doing what, and why. At least the one that is proceeding with caution is the one that practices respect and thoughtfulness! Everyone on this planet is different, and they all have different operating tempos, but it has been my experience that the ones that talk faster, or don't think before talking, are the

---

[27] One of the better books on the subject is *Science of Breath* by Harish Johari.

ones that generally have less integrity and less of a message to share. Of course there are exceptions to this, but they are only exceptions, not the norm.

Aleister Crowley has pointed out in several of his books that if you are walking down the street with a friend of yours, you will only know of him what you perceive. You will never know the complete him because you are not he. Working from this preface, is it clear how important language control is? I know I've stressed this multiple times, but I could stress it to the degree of Stephen King's novel "The Shining", and just write it over and over again to fill an entire book, and that would still not be enough. Language control is the most neglected magical tool in anyone's repertoire. As mankind evolves, so must the use of such neglected tools evolve with them.

Controlling one's breath can also have many physical side effects as well. For example, it can help keep the blood pressure and heart rate down. It also helps reinforce self-control, which is vital to success with speech control. Of course, this reminds me of a teaching from my childhood, when I was taught to count to ten before getting angry and saying something ignorant, as once again powerful teachings are hidden in plain sight. Breath control can also keep the lungs functioning at optimum capacity, and will promote proper circulation throughout the body.

## Speech and Anti-Speech

Let's talk about the anti-speech now, to truly address the subject completely. What is anti-speech? Well, it is silence, to be perfectly honest. What you don't say is as important as what you do say. Telling someone their options on a given subject is a lot different than telling someone what they can or can't do, although both may in fact be the same thing, simply stated in different ways. Most people I know would read the above sentence and think (or say) "Well, of course!" They are correct, of course, so if you find yourself thinking the same thing, know that I am aware of that. However, I still feel compelled to address this.

There is a level of strategy that denotes a certain amount of intelligence, experience, and wisdom. There is also a very clear statement that is made with silence. I have always learned that "sometimes, no answer is the clearest answer of all[28]". Talk about a profound statement! I have found that to be true time after time! And, as an expansion of that idea, I have found something else equally clear and sad but true. If someone responds to a question you ask with silence or avoidance, and you point that out to him or her, thus calling them out on it, **they really don't like that!** Anyone who very clearly gives you no answer doesn't have the ability to give a response to what you ask. True, they are making the choice to stay silent, but in that silence is also a hint at ineptitude of diplomacy. Sometimes it is because they are motivated by fear. Sometimes they are motivated by a self-feeling of ignorance. In any event, some people get very skittish and feel very cornered when you call them on it. Of course being the one to recognize this in someone and calling him or her out on it puts the querent in a position of power. Some people may see my above statement and disagree, probably very passionately. To them I offer this: Thanks for the passionate energy my way. I appreciate it! I'll just apply it where I feel it should appropriately go.

If you ask someone their thoughts on a subject and they don't give any answer then the tables have turned from a mutual and equal conversation to one where the questioner has the linguistic high ground. Why? All of a sudden they went, through no action of their own, from attempting to start a conversation with two participants (at least) in it, to a situation where someone is having their questions avoided. I don't know about the average reader

---

[28] I don't have an author or text that this is from, but I have learned this in classes. For more info, contact author.

of this, but if someone avoids my questions, I have a tendency to get irate. Why? Simple: I asked a question. I'm seeking a response. Who are you, the one being asked the question, to deny me my answers? What is it about me that you want to know, and do I want to share it with you? Are we going to tiptoe into boundary issues with this question? Do you think you're better than I am? If you don't think that, then what nerve have I hit on that you can't face? What issue did I just bring up that you are too weak to face directly? And why am I the one, in front of you, that you choose to hide from? So many possible reasons and outcomes can come from this sort of beginning of a conversation that I can't possibly cover them all here. If I attempted, I would be delving too much into psychology and healing topics and this is a text of language and language control. To simply quote *Zack de la Rocha* of Rage Against the Machine: "I know the power of a question."[29]

Does this mean that I get verbally belligerent towards them? No, not at all. After all, when one loses their emotional cool in a conversation, then they have lost the discussion, for they have descended into the emotional plane, which is lower than the mental, and the mental is where the clear and intelligent conversations exist. Yes, it is possible to be passionate about a subject and still maintain mental clarity, but I have found that to be the exception rather than the norm over the years I've been paying attention. Too many people confuse being passionate about a subject with being emotionally out of sorts. I have found this perception to be true for both the audience and the transmitter. Too many people that initiate conversation can't tell the difference, and too many people that are the audience of the conversation can't tell

---

[29] From the song "Fistful of Steel" off of the first RATM album: *Rage Against the Machine* Sony, 1992. No challenge to copyright intended. Actually, nothing but respect for these guys!

the difference. There are many reasons for this defect, and while a lot of the reasons are societal, many of them are also biological. For example, when our emotions get activated, it triggers an energetic response from our body, and for the average person it is hard to cut energy out from emotions.

This reflects a teaching that I have been working with over the last few years, which is the teaching that it is wise to honor the emotions without letting them dictate your behavior. For example, one of the things that I do if I am emotionally activated over something is find an outlet for the pent up energy, and after the energy is released, I'll revisit the subject in my head to look at it more clearly. This again is something that I learned in my youth. After the energy behind emotions is removed from the situation, we are in a better position to see clearly and to respond appropriately. Knee jerk reactions are almost never good when it comes to communications. Think of how many times we've seen public figures say or do something in the heat of the moment, only to apologize or backtrack on it later. It's actually more common than not, and while yes, our emotions are what make us human, our emotions are also one of the biggest areas for growth that we as a species have.

So, avoidance of a conversation has thus been covered. Now we will go to the next logical angle: silent conversation. Here I'm going to address body language and physical mannerisms. This will be a very brief discussion, but I feel a very necessary one. There have been many, many books over the years on not only reading body language[30], but also non-verbal communication, up to and including mimes and mimicry. If a proper and correct interpretation of non-verbal and verbal communication is analyzed in conjunction with one another, an accurate and subtle communication channel

---

[30] An excellent example of this is *The Naked Ape* by Desmond Morris.

can be set up between instigator and receiver. As I like to call it, it's the "I love you (whack!)" syndrome. If someone is telling you they love you, while physically beating you, then obviously their words don't matter. Cross-purposed conversations like this are generally not that extreme and clear. Most times it is a lot subtler, and the only way one sees it is to train oneself to look for it.

Here's an example to illustrate my point: Let's say that you are speaking with a person about a major emotional issue that you're dealing with related to spirituality, and that while the person you're speaking with has different spiritual beliefs than yours, the two of you are still close. While the spoken part of the conversation may go smoothly, there is most likely going to be a point during the conversation in which the person you are speaking to says something to the effect of: "I'll pray for you." In the conversation itself this is seen as a nice gesture, but after you have left the conversation you may discover the insidiousness that comes with that gesture. They will be praying to *their* deity-(ies) on your behalf, but if they strongly disagree with your beliefs, there's no telling what they will actually be praying for. Even if everything is on the up and up, they are still worried enough to offer to pray for you, and with everything that happens in life, we don't need any more worry energy sent our way than what we're going to encounter in day to day life! Worry energy is destructive, and it is only after we leave the conversation do we realize that the act they are offering is in conflict with their words.

I'm not supporting any particular course of action with regards to the situation listed above, or derivatives of said example. I'm simply trying to show how all encompassing a knowledge, awareness, and use of language can be. When one begins to take control of their language, the effects are not restricted to simply "second rate" concepts, or things that are not physical, but it spills over into the physical realm. As we as humans become more aware and conscious of our language, and control it to a greater extent, we are thus helping our brethren that are still evolving from other kingdoms into human form. The more people that exercise control over their speech, and are aware of what is pouring forth or coming in, the quicker this evolution comes. Evolution is an on-going process; all we can do is help control the tempo.

## Details

Have you ever noticed how vague people are in their speech? I have, and it has motivated me to be more detailed when I speak. A by-product of that is that sometimes it takes me longer to get my point across, but when I do, it's usually more accurate. Being precise and detailed in speech is something that I cannot stress enough. A major reason for this is just for conveyance of a point. I would rather be known as verbose and run the risk of using too many words rather than vague and open to misunderstanding. However, sometimes this works against me because people hear what they want to hear, and this often manifests as them thinking I said a word that I didn't. This used to really get under my skin, but over time I let it go and just started paying attention to who was doing this. This taught me who hears what they want to hear, and who hears what is actually being said. I could then adjust in communication or interact with them according to their behavior and responses.

Hearing what we want to hear (and we all do it) is something that seems to me to be in the human nature, and yet is one of the greatest obstacles we face as a species. If all that we do is hear what we want to hear, then miscommunications run rampant and we lose our perspective on the consensual reality we all create, and which we agreed to be part of before we came down into physical form. This perspective often times goes along with pragmatism. To some this may seem negative, but really it's just seeing things as they are, rather than how we want them to be. This doesn't mean that we can't make things the way we want them to be, but rather it means that when we're all on the same page, the changes that we desire can occur more quickly and on a larger scale. This paradigm is what we have to work with, and while each of us is experiencing it subjectively, there is a large part of it that remains essentially objective.

Through our control of language, we put ourselves in a position of power not only over ourselves and others, but also regarding the manipulation of the reality that we all experience. Take, for example, lawyers, judges, and other related fields. They all use words that have precisely the meanings that they want them to have. The phrase for this technical language in the law is "term of art", which is a word or phrase that has an extremely specific meaning. I discussed this earlier in this book, but I bring attention back to it now because a hallmark of those occupations is accuracy in words, and in burying messages in between the lines. For example, if there is a court ruling that says "X" is illegal, then what is also being said is that there is a long list of things that are legal, but the author is just not coming out and listing them. I learned a reason for this through astrology, and I lovingly call it the lesson of the Virgo. Virgo is a mutable earth sign that is down to earth, practical, adaptable, analytical, detail oriented, and often likes to be in control. Yes, there is much more to it than that, but I simply want to establish basic concepts that are applicable to this writing. One of the challenges that Virgos have to watch out for is that sometimes they can be too critical or detailed, and sometimes they can be too controlling and, again, too detailed. Often times Virgos plan for every eventuality they can think of, and their general intent is to simply be prepared so that whatever comes up, they are ready for it and have a response for it.

And that's where the problem comes in, and where I learned a valuable lesson. Guess what happens when you take the above approach? Yep, the unexpected comes up and wrecks everything, leaving the Virgo frustrated, or worse. What this taught me is that you cannot prepare for every eventuality; there are so many people on the planet with so many different perspectives and thoughts, it is illogical to think that we can foresee every choice, action, and subsequent effect that we may encounter in day to day life, even if we have a routine life overall. The professions that I mentioned above are similarly not seeking to pin down every precise detail when they use words that have double meanings, or words that may be interpreted in a vague way. They simply choose not to address every possibility, but rather to address what is in front of them. After all, consider this: If they took the opposite approach (making decisions that are detailed to the best of their abilities), then think about how much more extensive legal codes and procedures would be! Also, consider how much time, energy, and money would be tied up in treading the same ground over and over again, every time a tangential situation arose. It would not only be impractical, but it would also be detrimental and defeatist. The average person like you and I would wind up asking ourselves the same question each and every time: "We're talking about this again? Really?" True, the cynic might say we're doing that now, but in reality we are detailing new perspectives and aspects of things that have already been addressed in an order to define and clarify.

I encourage you to be proactive about how you speak so that you convey your point in a very detailed and accurate way. By doing this, you increase your ability to add details and vibrancy to your life, and you increase your ability to be objective when it comes to dealing with situations in general. It takes the same mental focus and discipline that has been mentioned before, but the payoff is something that can be of great benefit. Yes, it may put you at odds with a lot of people that hear what they want to hear, but to me that's a small price to pay for being accurate. Everything has a price in this world, and it is better to define our prices for success than to have them dictated to us. Life is a contact sport after all, and by being willing to fully engage in it through our language, we open ourselves up to greater successes in line with our true Will.

# Chapter 9
# The Power of Emotions

For this chapter I'm going to take a slightly different approach to language, and discuss the necessity of emotions and developing control over voicing them, along with techniques for defending your reality with language. I touched on this earlier, and now I want to revisit it for greater clarity and definition. When some people are angry, they will hit or destroy things. Some people will create things as a way to get it all out. I challenge the reader to use a different method: to think, and to use the thought processes involved as a weapon. Notice that I didn't say tool, I said weapon. Why? A tool is a passive participant in helping you with what you're working on. A weapon is something you have at the ready to use in a conflict-oriented circumstance. Here again, it's all in the metaphors, which are the building blocks of reality. So what's my point here, you ask? Language is an active, vibrant way to create. It is not passive at all.

Before I get into that, though, let me lay some groundwork, The practice of creative visualization and imagery is important to address. Using symbols and images to convey messages goes back as far as humanity itself, and thus has a rich history. As a matter of fact, it has been so widespread that it is commonly said that the subconscious mind understands symbols and symbolism a lot better than letters and math formulas. Symbols are the language of the subconscious, which means that if we want to affect change on a subconscious level, it would behoove us to use symbols and images rather than words.

This leads us to the next part of this, which is creative visualization. In short, this is a technique that uses images as focal points for concentration and focus. There are many different ways to do this, and the techniques are as varied as the number of spiritual paths on the planet. In the Western Tradition this has been used for years in the Qabala, and is known as Pathworkings. Pathworkings are studying a particular path on the Qabalistic tree of life[31] through visual imagery to connect with the teachings of that path. In recent years this concept has expanded into more mainstream directions, and many books by many authors can be found on the subject. When this is worked with routinely and extensively, it soon becomes clear that you can train your mind to think in these images, and to be receptive to images that you may pick up during your day to day life.

For example, when someone says something to me that gets my juices flowing and I'm taken out of my normal mental state of joy, the first image that goes through my head is of putting my hand on a scabbard at my waist housing a sword. The mental plane, which encompasses all things related to logic, reason, and abstract thought, is always a prime place to approach life from. It conveys that you are in control of your emotions, and that reason and logic are two effective techniques that you have at your disposal in your day-to-day life. Further, the mental is often symbologically portrayed with the sword or knife blade, which represents the power of reason to divide one thing from the other. Of course this is imagination, since I don't wear a sword in real life, but this imagery is very useful to me because it keeps me from getting too emotionally distraught, and instead helps me focus on possible justified responses. Of course I have to exercise caution and discernment when I do feel out of sorts over something someone has said, since violence (both physical and non) is rarely (if ever) the solution.

---

[31] The "paths" of the Qabala are the lines connecting the various Sephirot on the Tree of Life, and each one has a particular significance which you may wish to explore in detail if this symbol calls to you.

However, using this imagery keeps me sharp. I look forward to the day when my reflexive imagery changes, but that is a developmental stage of the human psyche, and of humankind as a whole. Besides, I think its kind of fun to think like that. And, it helps keep a foot in the door of the Akashic Records Hall.

The more that we individually think in terms of timelessness, the more we remove the mental boundaries of time. This is very powerful, and discretion should be used when using these techniques, but it becomes easier to access memories from past and future lives. The concept of fractured or hierarchical consciousness is something that I have seen discussed a lot in recent years, and bears investigation. The more that we work with symbolism and pictures to ingrain them in the subconscious, the more we speak directly to the subconscious, bypassing the waking mind's techniques of using logic and reason to understand and view the world.

It takes a lot of control and discipline to use a metaphor like that because of what it implies. One must be prepared to draw the sword or other weapon of choice, if necessary, and that takes a lot of courage. If you choose to adopt this technique, the first time that you get an opportunity to use such devices where the action is acceptable to you, consider it. Why? If you don't, then energetically two things happen. The first thing is that your integrity is shot in the foot, so to speak. You didn't do what you projected that you would do. The second thing is that you didn't defend yourself when necessary, and that projects a vibration of being taken advantage of, or worse starts to build a victim mentality!

Now I'm not espousing that one should use this technique often, nor have it as a first response. I'm simply saying that one should be aware of the complexity associated with imagery in general and how it applies to language. No matter how you create your reality, there will be those times when defending yourself verbally is necessary, and it is those instances that I am going to address in this chapter. It is a last resort sort of tactic, but one that all people should be aware of and consider if they are to engage in life.

To start off with, let's discuss how physical world situations will draw out the defense mechanism. In short, there are a lot of things that we will encounter that will trip our individual ingrained triggers. A lot of the time, the situations that will occur in our daily lives are brought to our doorstep for a reason. The reason is not always clear, but it exists nonetheless. Is it worth delving into the particulars to find it? That is up to each of us to discern for ourselves. I have found that each situation determines whether or not I'll look for its root cause. For example, if something out of the blue happens when I'm at work, I generally don't look for the big picture cause. I'm content to just respond. Why? It's work. I have two jobs where I'm working in a field I love, and I used to have jobs that were just filler positions. So, if something happened at one of the filler jobs, then I didn't look any further than the surface. If something happened that related to the two that I have that bring me joy, I do look further; those are much more important to me, and it's more important to understand them. Remember, to have control over the earth plane, you must come at it from the astral[32] and the emotional level. That means that to affect change on the physical you have to have an emotional charge to power it. I don't know about you, but the only things I have an emotional charge over in my life are my spiritual path and very few other situations. Obviously friends and family can get that reaction to a certain extent, but a filler job? No way. It's just a job. I don't view the jobs that I have that bring me joy as jobs. I view them as extensions of my path.

---

[32] Dion Fortune; the Circuit of Force. Already covered earlier in this book.

Do they require work? Of course, but it's not called "The Great Work" for nothing!

To understand and practice this takes a lot of work and awareness. If situations come up that allow practice of these techniques, and you don't catch the opportunity, then it's a missed chance. But, since nature abhors a vacuum, opportunities will be brought to your door again and again, especially if you declare to the universe that you want to improve in that area of your life. This is a loving universe that we live in and with, and opportunities will be brought to our doorstep if we choose to grow on our path.

## In Defense of the Realm

When defending your reality, there are many factors to consider. First of all, while justifiable retribution may be karmically sound, you will still want to consider whether or not you choose to burn a bridge. If someone verbally attacks you and your reality without provocation, then responding in kind is purely in the name of defense. But, if your reality is attacked and you provoked it, then karmically there is no clear ground to stand on. A defense is one thing. Manipulating the situation to set them up for a fall is another. Clear and concise language usage can prevent any karmic messes by preventing a situation from developing into one in which hostility develops. The more bridges that one burns, the harder life can become, as the consequences of cutting people away aggressively can be wide-ranging. Also, the more bridges that are burned, the more karma will have to be dealt with later on down the road. I'm not saying don't do it, I'm saying be careful if you feel you must. I would advise that you do your best to avoid burning them. However, if you feel they must be burned, then light them up and watch the flames from a distance.

One of the side effects of properly defending your reality is that it opens up a channel to empathetically feel to a greater degree. Since your mind is completely open and active due to the necessity to create your reality, you can sense things better and more accurately. On a subconscious level, this is taking a small step towards developing telepathy as an attribute of the human race. However, being tuned in to that level of speech control takes a certain level of faith and trust. It is very much taking on the archetype of The Fool from the tarot deck. You step forward, knowing that the next step will appear when it is time, and that you won't fall. I love the way life fills out.

Telepathy is something that is often misunderstood, or thought hard to develop by the average person, but really it is easy. The channel Alice Bailey has brought through extensive information about it, so if you're looking for more detailed information, I suggest you consult her book by the same name. Telepathy has been highly sensationalized by Hollywood and the media over the years, and thus, like so many other things, it is not currently misunderstood. Yes, telepathy is the ability to read minds, but it's actually easier than you may think. One of the best ways that you can develop this skill is to energetically open up your perceptions. This takes a lot of courage, but when it's done, it can produce impressive results. When you are cultivating the use of this skill, you do have to keep in mind that often people don't like it when you pick up on their thoughts, especially if you pick up on something that they don't want you to know. Many times I've picked up on someone's thoughts, only to have them tell me when I call them on them that they weren't thinking that. Later on, either in conversation or from other mutual friends, it comes to light that I was correct with my assessment, and they simply lied to me. This point shows the power that comes with telepathy. If this happens frequently, it tells us two important things: one, that we're pretty good at it, and two, that we should rethink how we interact with those people who so consistently deny our perceptions. After all, they're trying to deceive us, and regardless of the reason, deception is deception, and thus calls trust into question. By attempting to deny our perceptions, the audience is also trying to dull our senses. Usually, dodging what we perceive is done out of fear of some type, and fear is failure, as well as a sign of weakness.

When defending the realms, you must be emotionless if necessary. Sometimes you must defend your realm to the ones you love, and that can be tough. My first recommendation is that your best tool is subtlety. Use precision in your language rather than overt brute force. Since they are loved ones, it allows for a greater margin of success or error. They are generally more forgiving than others are, but you never know how they'll take it. After all, they are family!

In order to be able to defend your realm properly you must know, with great precision, the boundaries of that realm. I've covered this angle already in this book, so refer to those sections. Suffice to say here that, before you know the boundaries of your reality, you must be able to empty your mind to the point where you detach from your limited ego perception. When recognition occurs that you are watching the shell of your mind give life and force to your body, you will truly see more intense results from the techniques in this book. This openness also leads into the realms of those that believe we are all one. They have good things to say and I love them dearly; also, in my humble opinion, they are right. Boundaries must be tested from time to time as well, so remember: "Everything in moderation; including moderation". However, while we are all one, we are all also individuals, and this is a point that absolutely should not be forgotten nor downplayed.

## Better Pre-emptive than Defending at All!

The best way to defend your reality is to define your parameters to begin with so that issues of defense don't come up. Forewarned is forearmed. If you come right out and define something up front, then karmically you're pretty clean since the other person knows from the get go where you stand, and they chose to cross the line anyway. This mindset doesn't cover such heart-induced concepts as compassion and mercy, but it does clearly define your reality. I thoroughly enjoy using this technique, and try to improve on it all the time. It makes it easier for me to address problems later if I remember that the other party had been informed of the boundary and decided to cross it anyway. The most common response I get from people when this sort of situation arises is: "Oh, that's right, I forgot. Sorry." Depending on the circumstances and the person, I either pursue the matter like a rabid pit bull, or respond with gentleness and forgiveness. I have learned that there is no one set way to respond when it comes up, but rather that I must take each situation as it is. Treating each situation as unique is very good training to keep focused in the moment. We as evolving humans cannot judge situations that are going on in our lives now the same way that we have judged situations that have happened to us in the past. We may, at any moment in time, be the culmination of all prior experiences into this one moment, but we don't have to be bound by the chains of said previous moments and their consequences.

However, sometimes it is clear that the other person chose to ignore my boundaries, and in these situations I can easily deduce that they do not respect me, and thus I know where something of they are psychologically coming from, and can plan accordingly. In some ways this subtle clue gives me the high ground. Another perk of mentally processing like this is that it also puts one in the driver's seat as to whether or not they choose to share this insight about the other. It is not always wise to share these insights with people, as it may serve a larger purpose to remain silent.

By addressing these two issues at once, I feel that I am making up more ground developmentally than I would if I didn't look at things this way. I also feel that I am more in control of the moment, tapping into its underrated power better. The more ground one can make up in an incarnated lifetime the better! That means fewer repetitions in future lifetimes. That means fewer incarnations and more fun on the discarnate side! Further, the more perspectives and viewpoints we consider, the more we can be of service to others that we may come into contact with.

For language to truly be effective you must put emotional power behind every word you say. This doesn't mean "on the verge of tears" or "angry" every moment of every day, but rather to say everything with emotion backing it. Of course you can say everything flatly, with no emotions behind anything you say. This can be effective if you are trying to keep a low key, or currently practicing the fourth power of the Sphinx: "To be silent." I have found this technique very helpful when teaching me objectivity. When objectivity is mastered, then understanding karma and its right usage is right around the corner. As is a common thought in the Western Mystery Traditions, it is necessary to have emotional power behind what you do because that is the power that fuels workings. Therefore, in order to be highly effective in one's communication and one's magick, that emotional "umph" is a very good thing. The problem is that sometimes it is difficult to keep a clear head when that "umph" is present. A firm understanding of the balance between Hod and Netzach on the Tree of Life is very helpful here, as well as the path that connects the two: XVI:

The Blasted Tower, AKA War.[33] When this equilibrium is established, a firmer control is gained, and upward progress on the Tree of Life can be achieved.

Consider an old phrase that is very true, which is that it is wise to "have the courage of your convictions." Many people say they believe something, but when it gets tested, they recoil. This phrase, and the idea behind it, are two things that are very necessary to keep in mind when working with language as a magical tool. Before we speak, we should be well aware of the possible outcomes to our statements. If you think things through before speaking, you are preparing your ritual space before stepping into it. Thus the thinking through process could be seen as parallel to lighting candles, smudging, lighting incense, and other preparatory measures.

One of the keys to remember here is to use higher vibrational emotions when saying things, and come at things from those higher vibrational energetics. Not only can this awareness bring success where there were only barriers before, but also the ability to more clearly see results that show up. The view from "above" provides something of a bird's-eye perspective on reality, allowing understanding to develop from a less limited point of view. For example, often times people approach things from a fear based or disempowered perspective. I have seen many situations in the media where there is a change presented to society, and there is an immediate negative backlash, even though what is changed is displayed in a neutral fashion.

I intentionally look at the positive rather than the negative in situations like these. Recently there were changes to the IRS tax code that will affect ordained ministers, which will hold ministers more accountable

---

[33] In short, Hod represents the logical and analytical mind in the Qabala, and Netzach represents the intuitive part of the mind. When one is out of balance with the other, the path between the two, which is the Tower, is activated, causing equilibrium to reestablish itself, sometimes forcefully.

under the eyes of the law. When I learned this at a tax conference, I saw many people in the room almost visually shudder, but I smiled and embraced it because even though I will be affected in the way it will be more work for me, I also understood the necessity for such a mechanism in the law. Therefore, instead of shunning this out of fear or laziness of adaptation, I chose to raise my view to see the overall good and bigger picture, and made the choice to embrace what is best for the many at the expense of the few (in this case, the few being me). Outside of the United States there are many other examples too, but not living in those countries I am not really in a position to comment about them in a detailed fashion. Most of this mentality stems from the fear of the unknown, which the author H.P. Lovecraft wrote about quite extensively in his writings, and very accurately pointed out that is the oldest fear of humanity.

I don't know about you, but people that say negative things in a positive way constantly bother me. I understand why they do that, and not being judgmental I have no opinion one way or another about them, but I do have to wonder: "What is their intent?" Part of that wondering has to do with wondering about their integrity and quality of being. If I'm going to say something negative, I'm not going to come from a space of love and light. I'm going to approach it from a space that is emotionally neutral at best, and emotionally negative at worst, and I'm not going to be sorry for it, or make excuses for it. Better to have a clear message delivered than try to be something I'm not!

What a lot of people don't realize is the way that this entire topic is centered on self-control and sharp wits. Can you pursue some of these techniques without sharp wits? Of course you can. You just have to be as prepared as possible and not beat yourself up if you don't have something witty to say when a situation comes up that you didn't anticipate. The old motto from the Oracles rings true once again: "Know thyself". If you have a weakness in a particular area, then recognize it, accept it, and either improve it or let go of your judgment of yourself regarding it. You'd be surprised how much this simple procedure will reveal about you and your life. If you recognize a weakness within yourself and you are content to accept it for the moment and not change it, watch the reaction of people in your life. If most are accepting of that trait in you, then you are surrounded by higher vibrational beings. If most ridicule it or verbally or mentally abuse you over it, then maybe, just maybe, you're better off without them! It's like winning the lotto. Through this awareness and work you'll see who your true friends are.

One of the most disarming things that you can tell someone is that you know something about yourself that others may consider ethically sketchy, and you are accepting of it. The way that I have incorporated this into my life is to frequently (if necessary) use the phrase: "Yeah, and, so what?" Another phrase that I use often is: "Yep, I own it." When you show others that you know something about yourself that others may not agree with, and that you are okay with it, it puts the other person back on their heels and puts them on the defensive. This immediately gives you the high ground and the mental space to navigate the interaction successfully. This is just the tip of the iceberg regarding the sorts of things you can do with this thought, but I'm sure everyone gets the picture. By owning something like this, you accept the responsibility that goes with strong personal power, which opens the door for more opportunities for personal power to come your way.

To close this chapter out I would like to submit one final word on defending your realm. If you are defending yourself, not judging anyone, nor being unnecessarily cruel or extreme, then *feel no remorse*. Don't feel bad if you defend yourself and it hurt other people's feelings. Of course if you are going to an extreme to prove a point, then definitely feel remorse! It's like anything else in this world: Responsibility and Moderation. Defending yourself isn't wrong, but using a metaphorical nuclear warhead to wipe out a proverbial locust is wrong! True, you won't miss your target, but the negative effects of that action are far beyond what would have come about if control and discretion were exercised. I am all for a scorched earth policy when it comes to certain situations in life, but as I've gotten older I've learned to discern when it is wise to engage in it, and when it is not. While often it can be the most fun solution, it isn't always the most appropriate. The hardest part is not the determination between knowing when it is wise to lay all to waste and when not to, but rather having no remorse when you defend yourself. Because of the strength of emotions, people often times feel bad if they hurt someone, and while this is generally a good thing, it should be tempered with the awareness that you, as a human being, have the legitimate responsibility to *defend the self*. It is not that defending your boundaries should be enjoyed, it's that sometimes it simply needs to be done, and when this is the case, there should be no remorse. I have seen too many people feel bad when they had to defend their boundaries verbally to someone. It is good to have emotions and a heart, but if someone crossed you, then why feel bad for protecting yourself? I've never understood that, nor do I think I will in the rest of this lifetime.

Not feeling guilty when you defend yourself matures the mind and toughens the skin. If we continue to view the world through the same lens that we did when we were children, then we may become emotionally stunted if we're not careful. Often this is seen by psychologists and related fields as being indicative of an emotionally traumatized individual, and that is a point that I agree with because I have seen it true time and again. The general rule of thumb goes that if you can identify the approximate age of the attitude towards emotions, then you can also identify at what age the trauma occurred that caused the emotional growth to stall. When this happens, you are then in a better position to communicate with them because you can address them on their level, which should make things easier overall.

While this may seem like a tangent to a discussion about language, it is actually some of the most powerful material out there and can easily be applied to how we speak to others. By gaining this degree of insight into the behavior of others, we can better approach them, thus empowering ourselves to a greater degree of success when it comes to verbally creating our reality. This is also further proof that all things are related, and all it takes is a shift in our consciousness to achieve success. Most times this shift in consciousness is also an expansion of consciousness, which causes spiritual and psychological growth. I learned about all of this by learning about psychology to the best of my ability. Often, psychology and magick overlap, and if you're well versed in one but not the other, you may not recognize the true potency of your words and your own inner core. Part of what drove me to explore psychology is something that I learned as a youth, that when the Catholic Church actually goes to do an exorcism, a psychologist is required to be there along with a priest. I believe a medical doctor is also required. When I pondered that point, I realized the objectivity that they are perpetuating. Please keep in mind, though, that I learned that many, many years ago, so I don't know if that is still true today, but it is a fascinating thought to consider. This practice delineates things in a clear manner, and that is something that we've been discussing through this entire book: clarity. Applying psychology to our speech and ourselves can also help us remain scientifically minded, and through working with the method of science, we incur more growth than before.

Thickening the skin also helps us to handle whatever life brings our way. I do realize if you're not careful with this process, you may become too thick-skinned, which can lead to being jaded. While energy work is a good tool to use to not become jaded, there are others. For example, remember to laugh. If I find that I am taking things too seriously, thus becoming jaded in the process, then I go out of my way to watch comedic movies, or enjoy stand-up comic routines. In one way this keeps us young at heart, and in another way the physical act of laughter has been scientifically shown to be physically good for the body, thus promoting good health. There are, of course, other tools out there, so I encourage you to find what works for you. After all, when you find the proper tool to keep you from becoming jaded, you can then incorporate laughter in a better way into your day-to-day language, this raising the vibration of yourself and your audience. After all, it has been said that laughter is the unpronounceable name of god, and is the best banishing.

By being emotionally engaged in conversation, yet in control of said emotions, you can empower your words and ideas so that they can manifest in a bigger way in this consensual paradigm, thus living a life that is bigger than most. However, this must be done carefully, because if you're not careful, you can lose that emotional control, which of course can destroy everything that was worked towards. When one loses their emotional control, they have lost the advantage, and have actually opened themselves up to being wounded. Metaphysically, their light on the other side of the veil grows brighter, which can potentially attract those beings that feed on emotions. This can put the person in a very tenuous position, and can cause a lot of headaches in the long run.

All of us have this beautiful world, body, and lives to live. Sometimes it's necessary to protect that, but going overboard is not the solution. Use a hammer to fix a loose nail. Don't use a pyramid foundation stone. Besides, using a hammer is easier anyway! However, remember the saying that if the only tool you have is a hammer, then every issue is a nail, so it is wise to constantly add to your skill set and tools. The tools that would be wise to develop are not only confined to the vocabulary and speech, but also when it comes to emotions, emotional control, and emotional health. All of these tie together, and because of this, mutual exclusivity is not wise practice. Since emotions correspond to the element of water, and thus the astral plane they carry a more powerful charge than the physical plane. Because of this, they require more attention than the physical plane does. Most of this attention has to do with controlling them and staying emotionally healthy. If we're not emotionally healthy, it can be quite difficult to create our reality via language because we have a twisted view of what reality is. Nobody is 100% perfect and healed, but everyone has it within their capacity to heal and grow beyond where they started, if they so choose, and choose to put in the hard work it requires.

Using emotions can be a very dangerous thing, so if you were looking for a topic in this book to play conservatively, then this would be the topic. The use of emotions is something that can be very healthy and empowering to execute, but it will affect other peoples' emotions, too, and they may not be as well versed in working with emotions as you are; thus headaches may arise for a variety of reasons. When one begins to work with emotions, they also work with their speech, as the two are often intrinsically related. How one approaches emotions, especially when put into context of language control, can reveal quite a bit about the person's base psychological orientation and disposition, too. If someone believes in an "all or nothing" mentality when it comes to emotions, they you know that they are more extremist and polar in their views. Thus it can be logically deduced that they are not too interested in compromise, which means that working with them in situations that may require compromise may not be possible, or at least not easily possible. By spotting the motivations of people in how they work with emotions, we also further our control and skill with telepathy, for we start to move into the realm of being able to read between the lines, and thus silence becomes just as powerful as words.

# Chapter 10
## Making It Real

All of this brings me to my final point: Discipline. I've hinted at it several times through this book, but I would like to dedicate an entire chapter to it now. I see a lack of discipline sabotaging people's attempt to do magick more often than not, whether their efforts are verbal or otherwise, and thus I feel that it can't be stressed enough. All the books on language can be read, but if techniques aren't attempted, then experiences can't be gained, and skills can't be mastered. In this book I have given many thoughts on language and its magickal application. There have been many different ways discussed regarding how to create reality with just words and integrity. Now it is up to each individual reader to decide how to how to incorporate language awareness into his or her reality creation. Why am I bringing this up now so bluntly? It is a very simple principle: The more people that are actively working towards creating their reality from a spiritually wholesome perspective, the better we all are. To bring about a mass shift of consciousness, we need people everywhere, as many as possible to be consciously building a reality in accord with harmonious principles. The days of feeling like one is forced to play by another's rules will be on their way out. Slavery to another will be abolished through a mass realization that, through work, we can live how we choose to live, in harmony with Mother Nature and the Divine.

Sounds pretty tough, doesn't it? Well then I appeal to those souls that are more advanced than others in their insight into this concept to help their fellow humans who seek advice. Consider it a call to all Bodhisattvas everywhere! The time is at hand to act en masse. It is time to go forth and spread the word of reality creation through control of language. Now in this era of fear mongering and paranoia programming, the time is ripe for a spiritual overhaul. Everyone is already staying home more anyway, so let's make the most of it. What one believes in is only of secondary importance, because we all can agree on one thing: happiness is the greatest feeling of all. Whether through love, or through professional sporting conflicts, or other means, happiness is what keeps the peace. Therefore, tolerance must be exercised on all faiths, even ones that seem to be in conflict with one another. With a correct understanding of karmic and universal laws, we can all live in peace in our respective created realities.

### Journal It and Graph It!

The best way to track the progress on this path is through the use of a journal. Journal entries, and of course paying attention to the patterns they reveal, are the best ways to spot what is actually occurring around you. Of course recording these things doesn't do you any good if you don't review from time to time. Pick a schedule that works for you and review what is going on in a timely and rhythmic fashion. Through this, you also keep your mind clear and in the present. This allows greater communion with spirit, and through this, greater control of our individual vibrations can be achieved. In Spiritualism, the ability to control our vibrations is a definition of mediumship. This is extrapolated to mean that a medium is simply one that can control, alter, and change their vibrations in accord with their Will, and through this can contact beings, ideas, and concepts that don't necessarily come from the physical plane and its vibrations.

Through this book you have seen me explain and expand upon the concept of vibrations, so doesn't this add a little twist into the equation? When you put the pieces together, what it tells us is that every time you write and are conscious of the vibrations, you are *technically* performing mediumship of a particular type, as it is defined by Spiritualism. What or who you are channeling, though, could be debated for quite awhile. Some would say that you are channeling yourself, or your ascended self, or whatever being is floating around in your aura at the time. Ultimately you know what you are channeling, but let's face facts. Some people would doubt that you are even channeling anything at all, and I will admit I do see their point, and recognize it. No matter how you manipulate the information, though, if a Spiritualist definition of a medium is someone who can manipulate their vibration to resonate with intended vibrations, then any time that you've adjusted what you said to get what you want, you have been "guilty" of mediumship. I find that highly fascinating because it is further proof that everyone is psychic, but what varies is the degree and the specialty. Liberally, the same thing can now be said of mediumship: everyone is a medium; all that varies is the degree to which they have that ability.

Let's look at an example of this before we return to our discussion of journaling. Have you ever known anyone that is one way when they're sober, and another when they're not? You could easily say that they are channeling and/or influenced by non-physical beings. Volumes have been written on this, so I see no reason to discuss it further here, but as a tease, I leave you something to ponder: Why do you think people call alcohol "spirits?" Anyway, back to topic.

After you have established a routine of writing in your journal at a pace that works for you, then migrate up to the next step. When you have the discipline ingrained to record these events, bring it into your consciousness more by making it visible and interactive. Try using a dry erase board, corkboard, or some other item that you can hang from your wall and physically view. Put it in a spot that you will frequent. What will work best varies from person to person. Some people will put it near their bed. Others will put it in the kitchen above the coffee pot or the stove, or at their desk or work space. No matter where you put it, put it at eye level so that even if you don't consciously look at it, it is still in your subconscious awareness. That way, even when you are not paying attention to it, it is still paying attention to your mind. On it, write goals, visions, accomplishments, but focus on the non-physical ones. Choose ideas such as removing negativity from your life, changing your fortune in general, or drawing a different type of person to you. This is a derivative technique of creative visualization, so if this technique appeals to you, you can find many different books and other tools available to you to work with this more. One of the doors that this technique opens is to further work with the astral plane, because at least a subconscious emotional charge is created, and over time this can compound into greater emotional investment.

After journaling is mastered, the next technique to play with is to graph it. Get an astrologically based day planner or calendar of some sort and record significant things on it. When time permits, go through those days and check things like moon phases and void-of-course moons. Also look for different aspects between the planets. All of this may sound like technical astrology talk, but just a month of study or so of the basic elements will make these few observed facts spring to life. There are many good beginning level books that can help you with that. I recommend going to your neighborhood bookstore or "new age" or pagan friendly store and see what speaks to you. To name a few books on the subject: *Astrology for Beginners* by Joann Hampar, *Astrology* by Kevin Burk, and *The Only Astrology Book You'll Ever Need* by Joanna Woolfolk. See where the stars are when you notice significant results that began with a flick of the tongue. In this way you chart your spiritual evolution and reality control successes. You also put yourself in a position to put astrology to work for you, which increases your personal power.

Also, on a side note, pay attention to common traits of those around you, and get good at deducing where exactly common traits come from. Does the conversation always turn to religion bashing of some sort or another when you are with your friend _____? Or when you are with _____, do you leave the conversation by feeling like you've gotten something worthwhile from conversation? This is one of the toughest things to do, but paying attention to non-physical themes around you can assist in sharpening your ESP skills. We all have these skills, but like anything else, their specifics are unique to each individual person. By exercising control over your language, you will see social and professional circles around you change as you shift your perspective and focus your vibration. As is often taught, the first step towards developing psychic skills is to be aware.

One of my favorite ways to watch this play out is to become good with innuendos and double entendres. These are some of the best ways to really observe the impact because both techniques reference one thing everyone has in common in one way or another: sex. Both innuendos and double entendres are used quite often when it comes to the subject of sex, and everyone has an opinion about sex, even if it's "no, thanks." Of course, the specifics of the situation should dictate when these techniques are appropriate and when they are not, but I'm confident you understand what I'm saying. The above techniques are excellent for bringing people out of their shell and working as an icebreaker when necessary. If you are in a crowd where this would work to ostracize you, then you may want to think twice. Unless, of course, this is what you're going for: Then by all means do it! Shock value can be useful, after all.

## Reclamation of Personal Power

A more esoteric product of all of this work aimed at controlling language is the amount of personal power it can bring back to you. By using words more strategically, you are making sure that your boundaries are honored and that you are in the driver's seat when it comes to how others perceive you, and how you are received by others. There is a world of difference between "I said Friday at eight," "I said the day after tomorrow at eight," and "I said this Friday at eight pm." If the second example is used, it doesn't nail down a particular day of the week. Of course, if that "day after tomorrow" is Friday, all is good, even though it may not be perfectly clear outside of the immediate context. The key here is to be as specific as possible without looking like someone obsessed with details. If you are obsessed with details, though, then this book should come naturally to you! Once language is mastered, it can be used to accomplish a great number of things other than just "magickal" results. There is a lot of healing that can come with it to those that apply themselves in that fashion. As with anything else, repetition is one of the keys to making it happen. The other key is good ol'-fashioned discipline. Yep, psychological elbow grease is what we're talking about here. Any of us can have the best ideas and intentions, but if we don't bring them into being on the physical plane, they are only of limited value. This is a birthing process that can teach us a lot about ourselves, and about what it takes to be successful in the physical world.

The individual can also heal through bringing awareness to those non-physical things that have power which we are surrounded by practically every day. Make no mistake about it: these currents of energy do have substantial power. The power is in part in the number of believers and the emotional energy thrown into it. By choosing not to play the game, you are reclaiming Will if nothing else. And that is a very good thing to reclaim.

Discipline is usually seen as a pain in the a$$, but really, it's just another tool of being an adult. Yes, I said that, and I own it. I have found that the more someone is disciplined, the more mature they are overall in many different ways. By adhering to a regimen, one can create structure in their life. By creating structure, you create a vessel for the universe to manifest through. If we don't create a structure, then the energy from the other side of the veil flows wherever it can, particularly if we are active spiritual seekers. I don't know about you, but personally I would rather have a vessel for that energy to flow into rather than letting it run rampant willy-nilly wherever it wants to in my world. Yes, this is a control perspective on my part, but I have found that it is better to take control than become a victim. The ideas of control and discipline are not two mutually exclusive ideas, but rather they generally go hand in hand with each other. In order to increase your personal power, it is wise to become more disciplined in general. Through both of those tools, you become more control-oriented. It is important to remember that this doesn't mean to become a control freak. It is one thing to control, and another to be controlling. Yes, you can exercise control without becoming a control freak, but the secret to manifesting that successfully lies in knowing yourself, and knowing when to say when. By knowing when we shouldn't attempt to control a situation, we stay humble and focused on our path. On a less spiritual level, this makes us less of a jerk if we stay away from becoming domineering and managing others.

## Non-Physical Exploration

These things are the thoughtforms that are created from the emotional charges of people that have believed in them over the passage of time. The more people that believe in certain concepts, the more energy they accumulate. When you extrapolate this out, it becomes clear how, whether or not you believe in the Judeo-Christian God, it does exist because it is fueled by the energy of all of the believers throughout the centuries. Of course as this is true for that particular deity, this is also true for other deities from other belief systems, and thus we have the explanation of why all deities exist. Similar to mediumship, the only thing that changes is the degree of potency. Some deities are stronger than others because there has been more recent energy poured into them, and for others, their previous heights of glory are behind them. This can actually be very useful if you plan on working with a deity. Some paranoid people may say that this promotes conformity because it promotes working with the most powerful deity that fits whatever it is that you are doing, but to them I offer a converse point: most of the deities that we're discussing have been around for a very long time, and although some are more powerful than others now, others are starving for attention; literally. A minor deity from fifteen hundred years ago is sometimes easier to work with than a major deity from a hundred years ago. The weaker deity gets woken up when more people work with it, so it tends to manifest in bigger ways, and to show up more directly than the deity that is more powerful, but only over the last hundred years or so. Yes, these beings have sentience, and it is wise to remember this when you interact with them. Over the course of time they develop awareness, and the most basic desire of all beings: to survive.

Sometimes deities seem tempting to us, when it would be better to stay away, and often times we should stay away, particularly if our intuition tells us such. The easiest way to stay away from them (or conversely work with them) is to be disciplined in our thoughts and speech. This mindfulness is something that eastern traditions teach quite vehemently, and I agree with their thoughts. Being mindful of as much as I can be, I put myself in a position to see things clearly and in a more thought-out way, which improves my communication overall. Through this improved communication, I open up and unleash my personal power, which I then turn around and use for others. Anyone can use this technique, and the only thing that will vary is the amount of time and effort that go into it. No matter the environmental background, this can be learned when one dares to ask the question: "Can I do and be better with my life?" When that question gets asked, the individual dares to show an interest in doing better. The trick to navigating the tests is to remember the karmic laws and then remember the work that it's going to take to get there. Once mindfulness is cultivated, one can then be focused on controlling their speech. As all of this comes to a head, they realize the necessity of developing appropriate discipline. Then it's time to break out the elbow grease and get to work. The challenge lies in that what needs work is discipline and self-control, which don't come easily to some people. You **must** be willing to work if you want change in your life. This is a fact that is often times mentioned, and I couldn't agree with it more.

Thoughtforms also reach into the concept of emotionally charged words. Because of their influence, we learn how potent words truly are, which gives us more incentive to extend our vocabularies, which of course expands our world view and increases what we can take conscious control over when it comes to our personal paradigms. If you also consider the fact that through human evolution some concepts, deities, and words have changed or disappeared altogether, then you can also see how some of these thoughtforms can become dormant, often times forgotten in the sands of time. Sometimes we come across these by accident, and sometimes we find these intentionally when we go looking. Whatever the motivation may be, it is simply worth being aware of these entities so that we can understand the greater context of what we can do, and how what we do can tie into the greater whole. Thus we put into practice the Hermetic axiom of "as above, so below." There have been many books written on thoughtforms, so I suggest that to gain a further understanding of them the reader consults Theosophical and magical texts that are appealing.

One final note on thoughtforms though, and that is that in a lot of ways, there is a vampiric nature to them. In short, thoughtforms gain cohesion, potency, and sentience the more they are fed the emotions of their believers and users. Hence, when the emotional attention changes from one thoughtform to another, it in effect starves the first form. When this occurs, the thoughtform only knows that it needs energy to survive. Of course what often happens is that it goes dormant from lack of energy being sent its way. It does not completely dissipate though, which means that future explorers may come across these dormant entities, and we may find them highly receptive to working with us. This is one of the reasons it is wise to know the true roots of not only your own belief system, but also how many deities overlap and merge. When this occurs, you can use discernment in a more empowering way, and you have maneuvered yourself into a position to access ancient and lost occult secrets. This exploration can be turned into a real art form if it is worked with in a proactive, healthy and personally empowered way. There are a lot of dormant thought forms out there on the astral plane by long forgotten civilizations and belief systems, such as Atlantean ones. C.W. Leadbeater discusses this in his book "Astral Plane." By being aware of this we can gain wisdom from sources that other people may neglect, and through this gnosis, we gain a greater understanding of energy and vibrations, which are the two components to successfully using vocal magick.

## Discipline and the Tao

An eastern tradition that bears a brief elucidation here is that of the Tao (pronounced Dow, phonetically speaking). It is based on the holy book the Tao Te Ching. At its essence, what it is about is bringing mindfulness to the present moment, and encapsulates a particular way and approach to life. It is a Chinese text purportedly written by Laozi, and is very brief, but its wisdom is quite profound. I have found it quite useful when executing vocal magick because part of its teachings has to do with simply be-ing, existing, and being mindful of all things. Other than the obvious mindfulness that comes from the text, another subtle teaching that it issues forth is that of discipline, which to me has been the most beneficial part. In order for us to be mindful and present in the current moment we must have discipline of the mind, and ultimately of the tongue. If we are constantly paying attention to the moment, then we live in the moment, and I have found that through this awareness, we can achieve greater heights of discipline.

Yes, as stated before, discipline can be hard work, but once the work is mastered, discipline becomes a way of life, rather than something that is outside of the self. At first, when working with discipline, it may seem like we're working with something external, but with continued practice, that discipline becomes us, and thus becomes a particular way of life and approach to life. Through this transition of consciousness, we enter into a state of being that is more regimented, routine oriented, and mature overall. By meditation and reflection, the concepts I have laid out can become quite a powerful tool to the serious magician. A primal state of being is something that is cultivated through its study, and because of this, we bring ourselves back to a very pure state. When we reach this state, a lot of things that used to affect us in particular ways no longer do, and some things that we may have missed before become clearer. For example, if our awareness and behavior are in the ever-present moment, then we don't really tend to have overwhelming emotional reactions to things, which increases our self-control and focus. By cultivating the Tao within us, we bring ourselves into greater alignment with natural law, for we begin to see that ultimately, nature doesn't care what we emote. Aleister Crowley touched on this in his writings, making the observation that if we succeed or fail, live or die, the universe really wouldn't care. This paraphrase of a popular phrase of his hits the nail on the head, and basically reminds us of the greater natural world that we live in and share with other living beings. By being reminded of this, we can open ourselves up to not only humility, but also to a greater understanding of our role as humans.

If we have the ability to produce vibrations through speech and make changes in line with our Will using only our voice, then we are truly powerful beings, and with that power comes great responsibility. Through the practice of discipline, we own our responsibility not only to each other, but also to the world around us. By being disciplined in speech and thought, we cut away things that are ultimately detrimental. Through discipline we create consistency in our lives; consistency not just of speech and thought, but consistency of behavior. This consistency can create stability and structure, and by creating these two very powerful things, we create a launch pad to launch the execution of our will. I have seen many people that aren't stable do their best to enact their Will on the physical world, but usually they fail. It's almost like they built a brick house on quicksand. Without a solid foundation, we cannot build higher or better. Until such time as we create a foundation, we are still getting our water wings and fumbling around. However, once that structure and stability is created, we can then move on to higher vibrational goals and aspirations. This concept is encapsulated in the common idea of Maslow's Hierarchy of Needs, and I strongly encourage a review of this point. Maslow was a psychologist in the mid twentieth century who created a visual aid to help us all understand what drives the human psyche. I realize what I'm saying is a very simplified version of this teaching, but it is actually a very profound concept, since a lot of it has to do with magick and the execution of the Will. I have not came across any information saying that Maslow was well versed in the mystical arts, but that only serves to reinforce the universal nature of both his work and of magick.

Even if you don't know anything about Maslow's pyramid, much wisdom can be gained from contemplating the concept. If you're building your life, then one of the most powerful and ancient visualizations to use is that of the pyramid. To begin with, you lay your foundation, which is created through discipline and structure. After basic needs are met, you are then free to build as you see fit, in line with your Will. After you build the next layer, you can then move on to the next, and so on and so forth. No one is born a master, so patience is wise to use during this time and during the tests and initiations that you will undergo throughout your life. Too many times people get hung up on the results, not enjoying or appreciating the process that goes with it. It is very wise to enjoy the process of self-discovery and hard work that accompanies the journey that life is, because as the saying goes, it's not the destination, it's the journey. By enjoying the hard work and opportunities that come our way, we can learn to appreciate the little things in life that too many people often take for granted, which includes things like a roof over our heads, clean water, and other accessories that many people in the world don't have. Not only does this cultivate humility, it also cultivates perspective and works to keep the ego under our control and in check so that we don't become too egotistical. Staying focused and appreciative of the process also prevents against entitlement, which is something that is common.

Discipline in all areas of life can breed success through adherence to structure and routine, and when basic discipline is mastered, we can then move forward into higher vibrational states of being and of behavior to become, as Israel Regardie put it, "more than human." This isn't an ego trip, but rather it hints at accomplishing things that other people can barely fathom. Through accomplishing these things we show others that new and better ways can be had. And to think, all of this starts with control over our voice and discipline of our thoughts!

Earlier I shared a technique for discipline that included the concept of discipline through pain using a rubber band, and I would like to give another technique here: Boundaries. Often times people think this is as simple as saying no to someone, but there are other approaches. For example, of the best techniques that I have found is simply that of not offering a choice where no choice is intended. "Would you like vegetables with your meal?" is a lot different than "Which would you rather have for your meal; Carrots or peas?" While this may seem subtle, it can be potent nonetheless. By removing the concept of choice, we subtly guide someone in a particular direction, and if done responsibly, it enforces the personal boundaries that we all have and should use in our day-to-day life. This technique should be tempered with intelligence, though, for sometimes this is not the best way to approach things. Sometimes it is wise to offer a choice, and I encourage you to use your own good judgment when applying this technique. It takes discipline to be mindful of this technique because it doesn't necessarily come easily to some people, and a lot of times it doesn't come easily because of training they received in their formative years. With a creative mind, many tangent approaches and concepts related to this can be found and applied in day to day life so that we tailor make such techniques to our Will. All of the techniques in the world are only as good as the discipline of our mind when it comes to implementing them. While intent is quite powerful, doing the work is even more so.

In closing, this can all be summed up in just a few words. *Awareness breeds focus. Focus breeds consciousness. Consciousness breeds evolution. Evolution breeds healing. Healing breeds strength!*

I hope everyone has enjoyed this trip into the surface of my mind. May everyone be met with success and joy!

# About the Author

Rev Bill Duvendack is an internationally known astrologer, author, presenter, and psychic. He routinely teaches classes on astrology and the western esoteric tradition, and is available for astrological chart interpretations and guidance sessions of many kinds. He is available for divination readings using astro-dice and tarot cards. He is President of the Astrological Association of St Louis, a member of NCGR, President of Circle of Light Independent Spiritualist Church which he is ordained through, a member of the Temple of Ascending Flame, an initiate of the Golden Dawn, and a member of BOTA. With over 27 years of experience in the Western Esoteric Tradition in many different forms, including reading tarot for 21 years, Bill brings a grounded and practical holistic view to his material. His magical writings have been translated into several different languages. For more information and to contact, please visit his website at www.418ascendant.com.

# Get More at Immanion Press

Visit us online to browse our books, sign-up for our e-newsletter and find out about upcoming events for our authors, as well as interviews with them. Visit us at http://www.immanion-press.com and visit our publicity blog at http://ipmbblog.wordpress.com/

# Get Social With Immanion Press

Find us on Facebook at
http://www.facebook.com/immanionpress

Follow us on Twitter at
http://www.twitter.com/immanionpress

Find us on Google Plus at
https://plus.google.com/u/0/b/104674738262224210355/